FAMOUS FROCKS
THE LITTLE BLACK DRESS

FAMOUS FROCKS
THE LITTLE BLACK DRESS

PATTERNS FOR 20 GARMENTS INSPIRED BY FASHION ICONS

Dolin Bliss O'Shea

Photographs by Daniel Castro

CHRONICLE BOOKS
SAN FRANCISCO

I dedicate this book to my very creative grandfather, Norman O'Shea. You always encouraged my creativity as a little girl, and we had many fun adventures together. I wish you were here to see my latest creative adventure, this book.

Library of Congress Cataloging-in-Publication Data available.
ISBN 978-1-4521-2365-3

Manufactured in China

Designed by **Jennifer Tolo Pierce**
Photographs by **Daniel Castro**, unless otherwise noted
Models—**Jillian Lieber**, Stars Management; **Alexis Hutt**, Look Model Agency;
    Delana Motter, Look Model Agency
Producer—**Karishma Singh**
Makeup Artist—**Preston Nesbit**
Hairstylist—**William Soriano**
Stylist—**Pauline Montupet**

10 9 8 7 6 5 4 3 2 1

Chronicle Books LLC
680 Second Street
San Francisco, California 94107
www.chroniclebooks.com

INTRODUCTION 7

PART 1: GENERAL INSTRUCTIONS

PART 2: THE FROCKS

INTRODUCTION

The Little Black Dress. These three words conjure up so many fashion moments, icons, and silhouettes that it is impossible to pick just one style. The idea for this book was born with the versatility of the LBD in mind: I wanted to offer a range of silhouettes and styles inspired by little black dresses worn by some of the most beloved fashion icons of past and recent decades.

In *Famous Frocks: The Little Black Dress*, I have chosen ten little black dresses that defined a particular era and yet are timeless in their appeal. We start with a basic dress Coco Chanel would have worn herself in the 1930s. Made from a soft and luxurious wool jersey, this dress is meant to be a blank canvas for you to accessorize and showcase your personal style. The last dress is a sexy lace number inspired by Kate Moss's seemingly effortless modern style in the early 2000s. The dresses in between cover a range of styles and moods: Joan Crawford's elegance; Ava Gardner's sultry satin; Audrey Hepburn's sweet, full-skirted dress from *Sabrina*; Grace Kelly's classic dress from *Rear Window*; Mary Quant's inimitable mod mini; Liza Minnelli's simple wrap; Anjelica Huston's sophistication; and Princess Diana's crisp tailored lines.

I'm an avid vintage-clothing enthusiast and collector, so writing this book was a dream come true. It was my chance to design the dresses that I want to wear and add vintage touches as nods to the ladies who wore them first. The dresses included in the book are not exact copies of iconic dresses, but my interpretation of them. As a pattern maker, I felt it was important to me to design dresses that work for different occasions and fit into the modern woman's wardrobe.

For each of the ten little black dress projects, I also provide a colorful variation—because no one can wear black all the time! So in all, there are instructions for sixteen dress projects and four separates projects. The separates are timeless basics that you can easily work into your wardrobe: a flattering A-line skirt, a slim pencil skirt, a cowl-neck top, and a basic button-back shell top.

The book is divided into two parts. The first part covers all the general information you'll need to know before making the projects—basic sewing tools; a glossary of essential terms and techniques; and a section on sizing, using patterns, and cutting the fabric. At the end of the first part is a checklist, Before You Start, which is a quick reference list of important topics that apply to every project (such as standard seam allowance). Review this list each time you begin a new project. Use this first part of the book to learn new skills, brush up on techniques you haven't practiced in a while, or just for reference when you need a bit more explanation. The second part features all the instructions for the frocks and their variations. In the envelope at the front of the book, there are graded patterns for each of the ten iconic dresses. For each of the variation projects, I give instructions for revising the patterns to make the ten variations.

I hope this book will inspire you to make your own clothes and even tweak the dress designs to best reflect your style. Make Audrey proud and get started on your very own perfect little black dress!

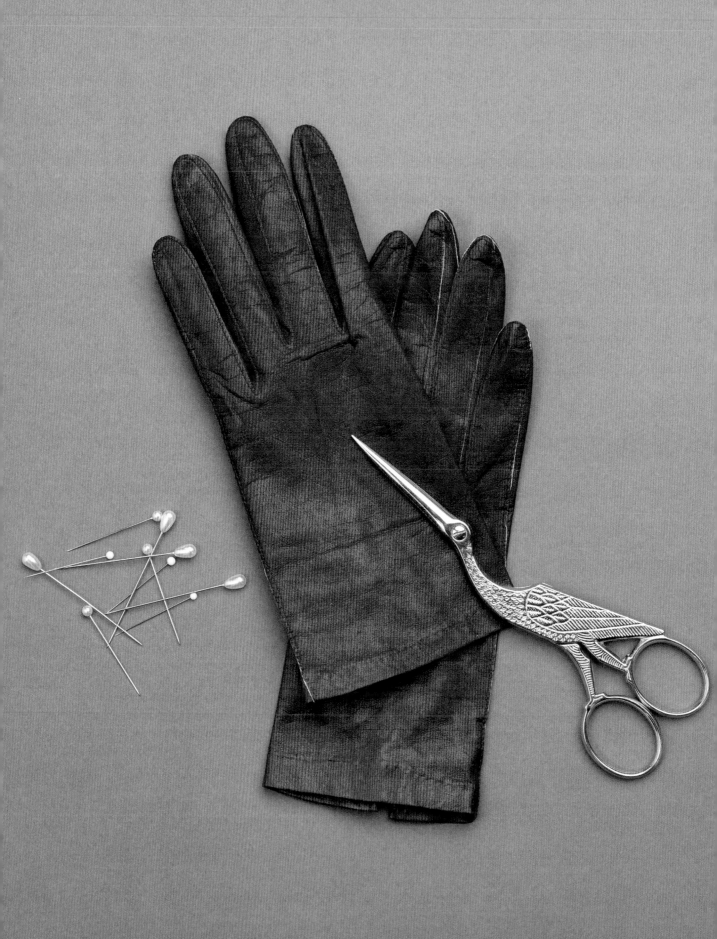

PART 1

GENERAL INSTRUCTIONS

TOOLS

Before making the projects in this book, you will want to have all the necessary tools on hand. This list includes all the basic tools you will need to make every project in the book. A few projects require additional tools; I've listed those items with the individual project instructions, so be sure to check whether extra tools are needed before getting started.

BASIC TOOLS

Clear gridded ruler

Dressmaker's carbon paper

Hand-sewing needles

Paper for tracing patterns (patternmaking paper, roll of paper for an easel,
large sheets of tracing paper, or a roll of examination table paper)

Pencil

Pins

Point turner (if you don't have one, a knitting needle or chopstick will work)

Quality steam iron and ironing board

Scissors—one pair for fabric, a separate pair for paper, a small pair for trimming threads,
and pinking shears (optional) for basic seam finishing

Seam ripper

Sewing machine—with a zipper foot, a buttonhole foot, and particular sewing
machine needles for individual projects

Tape measure

Tracing wheel

Water-soluble fabric marker pen, tailor's chalk, or dressmaker's chalk pencil

TERMS AND TECHNIQUES

This section of the book goes over some basic sewing terms, specific techniques, and some explanation of materials that are used in the various projects. The terms and techniques are listed in alphabetical order, so if you get stuck on a project or need more information, you can look it up easily.

BACKSTITCHING

Backstitching is used at the beginning and end of each seam you sew with your sewing machine as a way to lock the stitches in place. To backstitch at the beginning of your seam line, sew 3 to 5 stitches forward, press the reverse button on your sewing machine, and sew 3 to 5 stitches backward, then sew forward again and continue along the length of your seam. At the end of your seam, press the reverse button and sew 3 to 5 stitches backward.

BASTING

Basting is a temporary row of long stitches that are used to hold pieces together and can also be used to help create gathers. Basting can be done with a sewing machine or by hand. To baste by machine, set your straight stitch length to the longest length. Then sew as usual, but do not backstitch at the beginning or end of the seam; instead leave long thread tails. To baste by hand, make long running stitches (see page 19) along the seam line. Don't knot your thread, but leave long thread tails at the beginning and the end. Remove the basting stitches once you have sewn the seam together permanently.

Binding is a strip of fabric that is used to finish raw edges. There are many different types of binding for varied purposes. In this book, we basically use one type of binding: binding used as a facing made with single-fold bias tape. The Mary dress on page 109 uses double-fold binding on the sleeve; see project instructions on how to make this. Using single-fold binding as a facing, the binding is not visible from the outside of the garment and there is only a line of topstitching visible from the outside. This binding is used to finish the neckline and sleeveless armholes of a couple of dresses in this book. It could also be used to hem a garment, especially if the garment has a curved hemline.

MAKING YOUR OWN SINGLE-FOLD BIAS TAPE

1. Measure each edge that the bias tape will be sewn to, ¼ in/6 mm from the edge, and add about 3 in/7.5 cm to each of those measurements. Write these measurements down.

2. Cut a 1-in/2.5-cm strip along the bias grain (see page 18), for each of the measurements in step 1 {fig. 1}. If you don't have a piece of fabric that is big enough to cut the bias strip in a single piece, you can join the bias strips together with a seam to get your desired measurements. See the next step if you need to join strips together. If you don't need to join strips, skip to step 4.

3. To join two bias strips, if there is a selvage edge on any strip end, cut it off. Make sure each end of the bias strips you join is cut at a 45-degree angle. Place two bias strips perpendicular to each other, right-sides together, aligned along the short ends. Sew the ends together with a ¼-in/6-mm seam allowance {fig. 2}. Press the seam open, and cut off any points that extend past the long raw edges.

4. Press the bias strip into single-fold bias tape. The easiest way to do this would be to use a ½-in/12-mm bias tape maker (following the manufacturer's instructions). If you don't own a bias tape maker, using an iron, press the bias strips in half lengthwise, wrong-sides together. Then unfold, and press each of the long raw edges to the center crease you just made, wrong-sides together. When both of the long raw edges are pressed toward the center of the strip, you then have single-fold bias tape {fig. 3}.

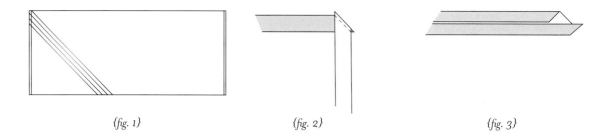

{fig. 1}   {fig. 2}   {fig. 3}

1. Sew shoulder seams and/or side seams as instructed in the project. With your prepared piece of single-fold bias tape, cut one end off at a 90-degree angle. Fold the cut end over ½ in/12 mm to the wrong side and press. Refold the long edges at the cut end along the creases and press them in place again.

2. Depending on the placement of the binding, the folded end of the bias tape will either be placed at the back neck edge of the garment or along the back armhole about 1 in/2.5 cm from the side seam. (See project instructions for specifics on placement and prep of bias tape.) Starting at the folded end, unfold one long edge of the single-fold bias tape and align the raw edges at the neckline or armhole edge, right-sides together. Pin the bias tape around the opening, making sure not to stretch the bias tape much. With the wrong side of the bias tape facing up, stitch along the first crease line, which should be about ¼ in/6 mm from the edge {fig. 4}. Clip the seam allowance around the curves (see page 14), being careful to not cut into the stitching.

3. Fold the bias tape and seam allowance to the inside of the garment and press along the seamed edge, leaving the second creased edge of the bias tape folded. With the raw edge of the bias tape folded under, pin the bias tape around the opening on the wrong side of the garment. Edgestitch, through all layers, along the inner fold of the bias tape, making sure there are no puckers in the garment fabric {fig. 5}.

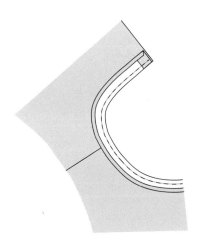

{fig. 4}

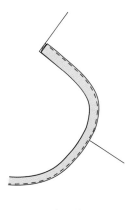

{fig. 5}

BUTTONHOLES AND BUTTONS

Buttonholes and buttons are a way to finish a closure on a garment. There are many different ways to make buttonholes, but the easiest way is with your sewing machine. A machine-made buttonhole is done with a narrow, dense zigzag stitch running down each side and a wider, dense zigzag stitch at the top and bottom of the buttonhole, and then you carefully cut a short, straight hole between the top and bottom zigzag lines. Each sewing machine is different, so check the instructions that came with your machine on how to make buttonholes. Where you have made a buttonhole, you will need to sew a button onto the opposite side of the closure.

Thread your needle, match both ends of the thread, and knot the ends together. Anchor the thread in the fabric, and sew up through the fabric and through the holes or shank in the button, then back down into the fabric. Continue sewing up and through the holes/shank of the button and back down into your fabric until you feel the button is securely attached. Knot the thread close to the fabric and cut the thread close to the knot.

CLIPPING AROUND CURVES

When you sew curved seams together, you will need to clip into the seam allowance so that the curved seam can lie flat once it is turned right-side out and pressed. If the curved seam is an enclosed seam (collar, cuff, armhole, or neckline with facing), first trim the seam allowance, grading the seam allowance if necessary (see page 17) to between ¼ to ⅜ in/6 mm to 1 cm. Then, perpendicular to the seam line, make small, straight cuts into the seam allowance on an inside curve, or on an outside curve, cut out tiny V-shapes from the seam allowance {fig. 6}. The tighter the curve, the more clips you will need to make. Be careful not to cut into the seam stitches.

Inside curve   *Outside curve*

{fig. 6}

DARTS

Darts are one of a few ways to create shaping in garments, and some of the projects in this book use darts. There are two basic types of darts: single-point darts and double-ended darts. Single-point darts start at a seam or edge of a garment, with the widest part of the dart at that seam/edge, and the end of the dart coming to a point within the garment, while double-ended darts start and finish within the pieces that make up a garment. Dart markings on a pattern usually consist of three lines: two outside lines that are the dart legs and an inside line that is the centerfold of the dart {fig. 7}. Sewing up darts is usually one of the first things you do after cutting out your project in the fashion fabric. It is a simple process with just a few steps.

SEWING DARTS

1. Transfer the dart markings from the pattern piece to the wrong side of your fabric (see page 37).

2. With right sides together, fold the dart in half along the centerline, align the dart legs, and pin together. Sew along the dart legs, starting at the widest part of the dart and ending at the point. Sew off the edge of the fabric at the point. Don't backstitch, but leave long thread tails. If the dart is double-ended, the process is the same, but you sew the dart in two steps: Starting at the widest part of the dart, sew toward one point, cut the threads, then go back to the widest part of the dart and sew toward the second point {fig. 8}.

3. Tie knots in the thread tails at the dart points and clip off the threads. For darts at the waist, on the inside, press the darts toward the center of the garment, and for darts at the bust, press the darts down toward the bottom edge of the piece. When pressing darts, I like to use a tailor's ham (a densely stuffed pillow the shape of a canned ham), which helps to press the point nice and flat without creating a dimple, which can happen if you press the dart on a flat surface. Repeat for all darts in your project.

{fig. 7}

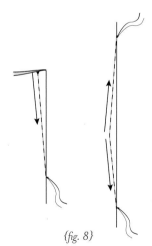

{fig. 8}

EDGESTITCHING

Edgestitching is a line of stitching placed ⅛ in/3 mm or less from an edge, seam, or fold. It is used to keep multiple layers flat, to strengthen a seam, or as a less noticeable form of topstitching.

FACINGS

Facings are pieces of fabric that fold to the inside of the garment and are used to help finish the raw edges of necklines, armholes, waist seams, and even hems. The projects in this book use most of these types of facings, and the project instructions will tell you how to sew them in. My favorite facing is the all-in-one facing that finishes both the neckline and armholes of a sleeveless garment.

SEWING AN ALL-IN-ONE FACING

1. Sew the shoulder seams of the garment and the facing together per the project instructions. Do not sew the side seams at this point (these instructions won't work if the side seams are sewn together).

2. Lay the joined facing pieces on top of the joined garment pieces, right-sides together, aligned along the neck and armhole raw edges, and pin. Sew the neck and armhole raw edges together. Grade the seam allowances, and clip into the seam allowance at the curves {fig. 9}.

3. Turn the garment and facing right-side out through each of the shoulders. Press the neck and armhole seams, making sure that the facing doesn't show on the outside of the garment.

4. In the final step, sew the side seams on both the facing and the bodice or garment. This step may happen at different times for the different projects, so refer to the instructions for when to sew the side seams. Flip the facings up at the side seams, so that the bottom edges of the facings are positioned above the armhole {fig. 10}. Align the edges of both the facing and the garment, making sure that all seams that intersect the side seam match (like armhole and waist seams), and pin. Sew the sides together in one continuous seam, beginning at the facing edge and ending at the bottom edge of the bodice or garment. Press the seam open and finish per project instructions. Then turn the facing back to the inside of the garment.

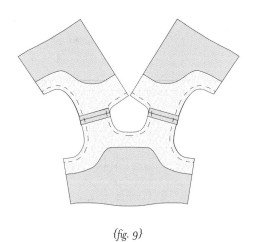

{fig. 9}

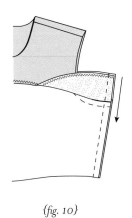

{fig. 10}

FUSIBLE WEB TAPE

Fusible web tape, or fusible tape, is a great sewing aid. It's so handy, I don't know what I would do without it. It is a strip of paper-backed web adhesive that comes on a roll in different widths. For most of the projects in this book that use fusible web, I used ¼-in-/6-mm-wide tape, but in a couple of projects I used ½-in-/12-mm-wide tape. When using the fusible web tape, please follow the manufacturer's instructions on how to fuse it in place. I use it to temporarily "baste" a centered zipper in place, and to hold hems in place on knit garments before sewing them permanently.

GATHERING

You can gather fabric to add fullness to a seam or a particular area of a garment and to create ruffles. This book uses gathers to add fullness and as a design detail. To control the gathering process and to get even gathers, I like to use three rows of basting stitches, instead of the more commonly used two rows.

SEWING GATHERS

1. With the fabric right-side up, machine baste three rows of stitching ⅛ in/3 mm apart. Place the first row along the seam line, place a second row next to the first on the seam allowance side, and then sew a third row on the opposite side of the seam line. Cut the threads, keeping the thread tails long.

2. On the wrong side of the fabric, grasp and gently pull all three bobbin threads at the same time, sliding the fabric along the thread to create the gathers.

3. Pin the gathered piece to the flat piece you want to sew it to, placing the gathered piece on top and distributing the gathers evenly along the seam, matching any notches or seams. Sew the pieces together per project instructions. Then remove your basting threads and press the seam.

GRADING SEAM ALLOWANCES

Grading seam allowances, or trimming down the two seam allowances to different widths, is a simple step in the garment-making process to reduce the bulk in the seam allowance. You grade seam allowances when both seam allowances are pressed to one side against the garment, like on a neckline edge that has a facing.

GRADING A SEAM ALLOWANCE

1. Trim down the seam allowance closest to the garment to about ⅜ in/1 cm.

2. Trim down the other seam allowance to about ¼ in/6 mm. You can use different trimming widths than given here, if you think it is necessary, but keep the wider of the two seam allowances closest to the garment.

GRAIN

Fabrics are made of fibers woven or knit together and these fibers form the grainlines of a fabric. There are three different fabric grains: lengthwise grain, cross-grain, and bias *{fig. 11}*.

Lengthwise grain: The lengthwise grain is the most common in garment construction. It runs the length of the fabric, parallel with the selvage, and is the most stable of the grains. Most woven fabrics don't have any stretch along the lengthwise grain, while knits can have no stretch or a lot of stretch along this grain.

Cross-grain: The cross-grain runs across the width of the fabric, from selvage to selvage. The cross-grain of a woven fabric can have a tiny bit of stretch, but it is not as stretchy as the bias grain. The cross-grain of a stable knit fabric is usually where most of the stretch can be.

Bias: The bias grain line runs at a 45-degree angle to the lengthwise grain and cross-grain. Most fabrics have some stretch along the bias grain. Designers have used this stretch to their advantage for years. Think of those fluid figure-hugging dresses of the 1930s.

GRAINLINE

The grainline on a pattern piece is the double-ended arrow line, which can be placed on any of the three fabric grains. The grainline helps you align the pattern along the correct grain of the fabric for the piece you are cutting. Where the grainline is placed on the pattern piece determines the grain of the fabric piece when it is cut. For the projects in this book, you will always align the grainline on the pattern so that it is parallel with the selvage edge of the fabric.

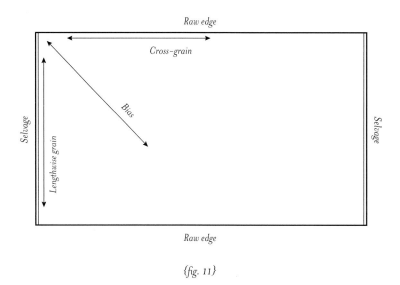

{fig. 11}

Hand sewing is an essential part of couture sewing. It is a good idea to learn some basic hand stitches, and who knows, you may enjoy the meditative qualities of sewing by hand so much that you make an entire garment this way. Don't laugh; it is doable. I have made quite a few wedding dresses by hand, including my own, using the sewing machine only to restitch seams that will be stressed. Once you start hand sewing, you realize that you have a lot more control over the fabric than you do with a sewing machine. I include only a few of the many types of hand stitches here, since I used these stitches in some of the projects in the book. If you want to learn more, see Resources at the back of the book or check out any book on couture sewing. The hand stitches included in the following discussion use only a single strand of thread, not doubled-up thread like you would use to sew on a button or a hook and eye.

Backstitch: The backstitch is a very strong stitch to use and is suitable for sewing seams together. I use it in this book to tack facings to the seam allowance at side and shoulder seams, not to sew entire seams together. To backstitch, anchor the thread at the back side of your fabric, and pull it up to the top of the work. Make a small stitch to the right of the working thread and pull the needle down to the back of the work. Pull the needle up to the left of the working thread, about the same stitch length as the stitch made to the right. Continue making small stitches backward, bringing the needle up to the front of each stitch. {*fig. 12*}

Running stitch: The running stitch is the most basic of hand stitches. It isn't a strong stitch and is most often used to baste two pieces together; it is sometimes referred to as a "basting stitch." To make a running stitch, anchor your thread at the back of the work and pull the needle up to the top of the work. Make a stitch to the left of the working thread, down to the back of the work, then bring the needle back up to the top of the fabric at equal intervals. You can make a few stitches at a time by rocking the needle up and down through the fabric, before pulling the thread through. {*fig. 13*}

Slipstitch: The slipstitch is the least visible of the hand stitches and isn't terribly strong, but it is a great stitch for holding two layers flat against each other, like a hem, or for attaching facings to each side of a zipper tape. To make a slipstitch, anchor the thread by putting the needle inside the fold of the top layer of fabric and bring the needle out through the edge of the fold. Take a small stitch (just a thread or two of the garment fabric) in the fabric piece you are joining the fold to, then insert the needle back into the fold and repeat. If you are sewing with seam binding that doesn't have a fold, you would sew the same way, but the stitches on the top layer would be visible since there is no fold to hide the stitches in {*fig. 14*}.

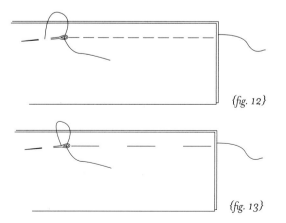

{*fig. 12*}

{*fig. 13*}

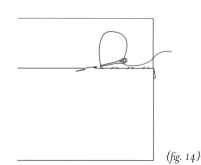

{*fig. 14*}

There are many different ways to hem your garments. I have included three of my favorites in this book; they are simple and easy to do. But by all means, if you prefer a different type of hemming technique, feel free to use it. If you do use a different type of hem, remember that you may need to adjust the hem width on your traced pattern.

BABY HEM

A baby hem is a very narrow hem that is good to use on thin fabric, on a rounded or flared hemline, and on linings. It is simple to do, but does require that you sew around the circumference of the hem a few times.

1. Sew a line of stitching ⅜ in/1 cm from the raw edge you want to hem. Along the stitch line, fold and press the hem over to the wrong side {fig. 15}.

2. Sew around the hem ⅛ in/3 mm from the folded edge. Trim off the excess hem fabric as close to the stitching as possible, being careful not to cut into the stitched line {fig. 16}. Fold and press the hem over again to the wrong side along the second stitched line.

3. Sew again around the hem ⅛ in/3 mm from the folded edge {fig. 17}.

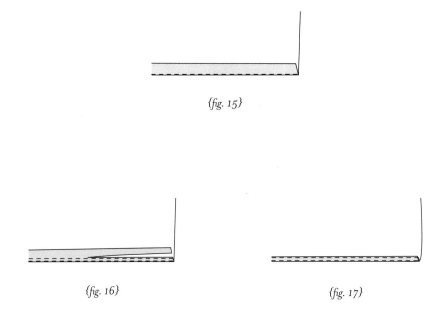

{fig. 15}

{fig. 16}

{fig. 17}

BLIND HEMMING WITH SEAM BINDING OR LACE

Blind hemming is a lovely finish that is almost invisible on the outside of a garment. It can be done by machine, but I feel you have more control when you do it by hand. This type of hem is best done on a straight or very slightly curved hem. You don't have to use seam binding or lace to do this hem, but you will need to finish the raw edge of the fabric in some way before sewing the hem. I love the vintage look of adding seam binding or lace, so the following instructions include this step.

1. Press the hem in place, following the instructions in the project.

2. Pin seam binding flat along the raw edge, with right-sides facing up, overlapping the edge by about ¼ in/6 mm. Machine stitch the seam binding in place along the lower edge of the overlap. When you get to the end of the hem, press under the short end of the seam binding to finish the raw edge.

3. Slipstitch (see page 19) the seam binding to the inside of the garment, making sure to only catch a thread or two of the garment fabric {fig. 18}.

NARROW CLEAN-FINISH HEM

This hem is simple and looks great on the inside of a garment because the raw edges are enclosed in the fold. It works best on straight or slightly curved edges. This hem can also be made with wider measurements; I use the following measurements in the projects in this book.

1. Fold and press the raw edge over ¼ in/6 mm, wrong-sides together. Then fold and press the edge over again ⅜ in/1 cm.

2. Edgestitch along the inner folded edge to stitch the hem in place {fig. 19}.

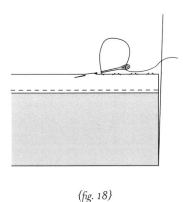

{fig. 18}

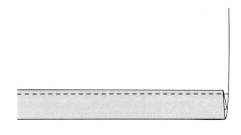

{fig. 19}

INTERFACINGS

There are so many different types of interfacing, it can be confusing to choose one for your projects. I like to keep it simple. I prefer sew-in interfacing, and there are a lot of options for sew-in interfacing. If you prefer working with fusible interfacing, be sure to test how the garment fabric and fusible interfacing work together once fused. You want to make sure that the fusible adhesive doesn't bleed through to the right side of the garment fabric. And do check whether the fusible interfacing is giving the fabric the support you are looking for. Here are some tips to help you choose the right interfacing for the projects in this book.

- The interfacing yardage given in the projects is 20 in/50 cm wide, since this is the fabric width most widely available. This consistency will make it easier for you to make your calculations.

- Remember that the interfacing will be washed along with the garment, so it needs to be compatible with how you will be laundering your garment. Sew-in interfacing fabric should be pretreated along with your garment fabric, before cutting. Fusible interfacings can be tricky to pretreat, but I have heard that you can gently hand wash and air dry fusible interfacing before using. The manufacturer's instructions should state how the fusible interfacing should be laundered.

- Choose an interfacing that has a weight that is similar to your garment fabric.

- I like to use lightweight muslin with cotton and linen garments, silk organza with lightweight or sheer silks, and lightweight woolens and taffeta with heavier weight silks or woolens. Cut these interfacing fabrics on the same grain as the garment fabric.

- If you use fusible interfacing, follow the manufacturer's instructions on how to fuse it to your garment fabric.

- Sometimes fusible interfacing can shrink your garment fabric a little bit, so when using it, I fuse it to the fabric before cutting out the pattern piece.

BASTING SEW-IN INTERFACING

1. Cut out the interfacing and garment fabric from the pattern piece that calls for interfacing.

2. Baste (by machine or by hand) the interfacing to the wrong side of the fabric, along all edges within the seam allowance. These two pieces will now be considered one.

KNIT FABRICS

I love working with knit fabrics and find them very easy to sew with. Knit fabric projects usually sew together faster, and I find that there are fewer fit or adjustment issues. The knit fabrics used in this book are considered the more stable knit fabrics—medium-weight jersey, double knit, matte jersey, and ITY (interlock twist yarn) jersey. For the projects that require knit fabrics, look for medium-weight fabrics with most of the stretch in the fabric along the cross-grain. It's okay for the fabrics to have some lengthwise stretch, but not too much. Stay away from sweater knits, really thin slinky knits, rib knits, or knits that have an equal amount of stretch along the cross-grain and lengthwise grain (like swimsuit fabrics).

Sewing with knit fabrics takes some experimenting with the type of stitch used, stitch length, stitch width, and even presser foot pressure. You don't need a serger machine (a serger sews and finishes the edges of a seam all at once) to sew knits, although it does make it easier. A basic sewing machine that has zigzag capabilities can make fine knit-fabric garments. I prefer using my serger when sewing knit garments, but in this book the instructions are written for a basic sewing machine. If you do have a serger, feel free to use it to sew your projects.

Before getting started on sewing with knits, make sure you use a sewing machine needle called a ball-point or jersey needle, specifically for knits (needle size 70/10 will work for the projects in this book). These needles have a blunt point that is made to go between the fabric's fibers, whereas a universal or sharp needle can pierce the fabric fibers, causing tiny holes along your seams (ask me how I know). If you are using a serger, choose a needle that is also specific to your knit fabric.

SEWING KNIT FABRIC SEAMS

I have found that a narrow zigzag stitch (on the sewing machine, set to width 2 and length 2) can be used on most knit-fabric seams. So that is my starting point when testing out sewing with a new knit fabric. Most newer machines have fancier knit-specific stitches that you can use and try out for yourself. I don't use these stitches much and they are more difficult to rip out if you make a mistake. For horizontal seams like shoulder or waist seams, which need more strength, I like to do double-stitched seams. To do this, make a zigzag seam line at the specified seam allowance, and then run a second row of zigzag stitches within the seam allowance about ⅛ in/3 mm from the first row. For most vertical seams, you can get by with just a single row of narrow zigzag, but on a particular seam that will be stressed, you may want to do a double-stitched seam. Once the seam is sewn, trim the seam allowance down to about ⅜ in/1 cm wide to reduce bulk.

There are many different ways you can finish a neckline and the armhole edges on a knit garment. For this book, we will use two of my favorites, single-layer binding and binding as a facing. Single-layer binding is a binding that is visible on both the outside and inside of the garment. It wraps around a raw edge, and for these projects, stretches with the garment. Binding as a facing is only visible from the inside and for our purposes is a more stable, less stretchy option. In this case, you see the topstitching that holds the binding as a facing in place from the outside.

Single-Layer Binding (Not Really a Single Layer)

1. Cut the binding strips along the cross-grain, and make them four times the width of the finished binding. For this book, all the single-layer binding finishes are ⅜ in/1 cm wide, so cut a strip of fabric 1½ in/4 cm wide along the cross-grain. Cut a strip that is long enough to go around the neck or armhole edges.

2. It is best to sew binding to a flat opening. On a neck edge, sew just one of the shoulder seams together per project instructions, or for an armhole, sew just the shoulder seam together and leave the side seam open.

3. Sew binding to a neck or armhole opening. With right-sides together, with the binding on top and raw edges aligned, sew the binding in place using a narrow zigzag stitch and a ⅜-in/1-cm seam allowance. While sewing around the curves, slightly stretch the binding piece only, making sure not to stretch the neck or armhole of the garment. Since the binding piece is on top, you can stretch it slightly while letting the machine feed the neck or armhole of the garment through. You also don't want to stretch the binding so much that it makes

the neck or armhole pucker. Press the binding toward the raw edges. Trim off any excess on the binding ends so they are even with the garment edges {fig. 20}.

4. Sew the remaining shoulder seam or side seam together per project instructions. Keeping the binding pressed toward the opening, align the binding raw edges and match at the binding seam before sewing the shoulder or side seam together.

5. Fold the binding over the raw edges to the wrong side of the opening and press in place. The binding should easily cover the stitching from step 3. From the right side of the garment, pin the raw edge of the binding in place around the opening.

6. Using a narrow zigzag stitch (width 1 to 1.5) and with the right side facing up, edgestitch around the inner folded edge of the binding, making sure to catch the single layer of binding underneath. Press, and on the inside of the opening, trim the binding raw edge close to the stitching {fig. 21}.

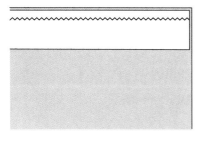

{fig. 20}

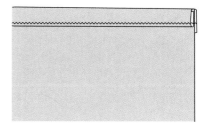

{fig. 21}

Binding as a Facing with Knit Fabric

1. Cut strips of fabric on the lengthwise grain (which is less stretchy in the knit fabrics used for the projects in this book) four times the width of the finished facing. For this book, all the facings finish at ½ in/12 mm, so cut a strip of fabric 2 in/5 cm wide along the lengthwise grain. Then press the strips in half lengthwise. Cut a strip that is long enough to go around the neck or armhole edges.

2. It is best to sew the facing to a flat opening. For an armhole, sew just the shoulder seam together and leave the side seam open. The projects in this book that have this treatment on the neck edge have an open neckline, so you will sew both shoulder seams together per project instructions.

3. Sew the facing to the neck or armhole opening. With right-sides together, folded facing strip on top, and raw edges aligned, sew the facing in place using a narrow zigzag stitch and a ⅜-in/1-cm seam allowance {fig. 22}. While sewing around any curves, slightly stretch the facing piece only, making sure to not stretch the neck or armhole of the garment. Since the facing piece is on top, you can stretch it slightly, while letting the machine feed the neck or armhole of the garment through. You don't want to stretch the facing so much that it makes the neck or armhole pucker.

4. Press the facing piece toward the raw edges. With the garment right-side up, understitch (see page 33) the seam allowance layers to the facing, close to the seam, using a straight stitch. Then trim off about ⅛ in/3 mm from the seam allowance raw edges. Cut off any excess on the ends of the facing strip so that they are even with the garment edges {fig. 23}.

5. For the armhole facing only, sew the side seam together per project instructions. Keeping the facing pressed toward the opening, align the facing folded edges and match at the facing seam before sewing the side seam together.

6. Fold the facing and seam allowance edges to the wrong side of the opening and press in place. Pin the folded edge of the facing over the raw edges of the seam allowance.

7. You have a few options on this last step, depending on the amount of stretch the fabric has. For stretchy fabrics, use a narrow zigzag stitch (width 2): With the wrong side of the garment facing up, edgestitch the inner folded edge of the facing in place, then press {fig. 24}. On thinner, more stable (less stretchy) fabrics, you can also use a twin needle (a special type of needle that has two needle tips mounted onto a single shaft and fits into your machine) for this step, but sew the facing in place with the right side of the garment facing up. If the fabric is stable and doesn't stretch much, you can use a straight stitch. To establish how your fabric will work with the stitching choices, test the different options on fabric scraps; you want to make sure your stitching stretches with the fabric and doesn't break.

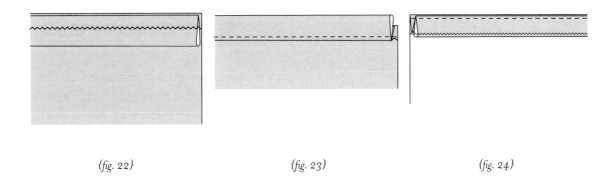

{fig. 22}   {fig. 23}   {fig. 24}

This can be one of the biggest challenges for folks sewing with knits, since it is a bit more work to get the same look as a ready-to-wear hem. Most store-bought knit garments are hemmed with a specific machine, called a coverstitch machine. They now sell home sewing machines that just do a coverstitch (some serger machines even have this capability), but most folks don't own one. You can get this same look by using a twin needle in your machine and both top threads in the same color. Following is my process for hemming a knit fabric. You can either use a twin needle with a straight stitch or a narrow zigzag stitch in step 3. Be sure to test whichever stitching method you use; you want your hem to stretch with the garment without the stitches breaking. When using a twin needle, you might need to lengthen your straight stitch length a bit so you don't get skipped stitches.

1. Press the specified hem width to the wrong side of your fabric. Knits usually don't hold a pressed crease well, but it is good to do this step so you have some sort of crease line to follow.

2. Unfold the hem and lay ¼-in/6-mm fusible web tape (see page 17), tacky-side down, along the raw edge of the wrong side of the fabric. Finger-press the tape in place. Remove the paper backing, refold the hem along the crease, and finger-press the hem in place. With the iron, lightly press along the hem, to adhere the fusible tape to the garment.

3. With the right side of the garment facing up and your machine set to straight stitch with a slightly longer stitch length (around length 3 for my machine) or a narrow zigzag stitch, sew around the perimeter of the hem about ⅛ in/3 mm from the raw edge of your hem. For example, if the hem width is ¾ in/2 cm, stitch ⅝ in/16 mm from the folded edge of the hem. When starting and stopping the stitching on a hem, I don't backstitch; I just overlap the beginning stitches 1 to 1½ in/ 2.5 to 4 cm with the ending stitches. To me this makes a neater and less noticeable hem.

A lining can serve many beneficial purposes in garments: it can make a sheer garment less sheer, add comfort to a stiff or scratchy garment, hide the seam allowances, add some stability to the garment's fabric, and help a garment skim your body instead of clinging to it. For some garments, you do not need to line the entire garment. For example, on a full-skirted dress, I may only line the bodice, since it is right against my skin. In this case, the lining helps keep the garment fabric clean while providing extra stability to the tight-fitting bodice. For some garments, you may not want to line them at all and just wear a slip underneath. I often do not line summer garments. There are different fabrics you can use as lining. For the projects in this book, you will want a smooth, lightweight fabric—a popular choice is Bemberg rayon.

HOW TO LINE A DRESS

1. Cut out the lining fabric using the bodice and skirt pattern pieces for the project you are making.

2. You can decide to not use the facings at this point if your lining matches your dress fabric, or keep the facings if your lining is a different color from your dress. If you keep the facings in the dress, there is no need to interface your facing pieces, since the lining will act as your interfacing. Press the bottom raw edges of your facings under, to the wrong side, about ¼ in/6 mm, align the facing and lining raw edges, right-sides up, and pin them together. Edgestitch (see page 16) the facing hem in place on the lining and baste both layers together along the raw edges within the seam allowance; these layers will now be treated as one.

3. Sew the lining pieces together in the same way that the dress fabric pieces are sewn together. If your dress is sleeveless, follow the instructions for sewing an all-in-one facing (see page 16) to sew the lining to the bodice neck and armholes. If your dress has sleeves, sew the lining to the bodice neck, right-sides together, then flip the lining to the wrong side of the bodice, press and grade the neck seam allowances toward the lining, and understitch (see page 33) around the neck. Then baste the lining and bodice armholes together within the seam allowance. Insert the zipper per the project instructions. Turn under the lining edges at the zipper, and slipstitch the lining to the zipper tape.

4. Cut the lining bottom edge about 1 in/2.5 cm shorter than the skirt, and hem the lining with a baby hem (see page 20).

NOTCHES

Notches are small triangles that are printed on the edge of a pattern piece. They are used as match points, to know where a zipper ends, or where to put gathers. To mark where the notches should be cut on your fabric, take a look at the pattern piece. Where you see a small triangle along the cut line for your size, that is where you should make a small clip in the center of the triangle, into your seam allowance, about ¼ in/6 mm long.

PIVOTING

Pivoting in sewing is when you want to change your direction of sewing but don't want to stop your line of stitching, like sewing around a corner. To pivot, drop your sewing machine needle into your fabric where you want to pivot, raise the presser foot, rotate the fabric in the direction you want to sew, drop the presser foot, and continue sewing. Sometimes it is hard to eyeball where to pivot and maintain the same seam allowance, so I either mark my pivot point with a pin (removing pin right before the presser foot reaches it) or draw a dot with a fabric marker/chalk pencil on the fabric.

PRESSING

Pressing and ironing are two different actions you do with your iron. To press, you place the iron on your fabric and apply pressure, then pick up and move the iron to the next position on a seam or hem that needs to be pressed. To iron, you move the iron back and forth on your fabric without picking it up. When constructing a garment, you want to press, not iron.

There are so many types of seams and seam finishes, but I won't cover them all in this book. Here are the seams and finishes used in these projects.

Princess Seams

Princess seams add shaping to a garment. They run vertically down a garment, breaking up the front and back into three pieces (or more if there is a center seam). Princess seams can be placed to start along the shoulder seams, armholes, or even the neckline and continue down to the bottom edge or waist seam. They are flattering seams that can be contoured to get a very close fit, or can be made straighter for a looser fit. When you first start sewing princess seams, you may find them tricky because you are sewing together two pieces that have opposing curves, and there is usually ease built into the front princess seam. I have found that princess seams are a cinch to sew if you do a little prep work to the pieces first.

Sewing Princess Seams

Note: *For all of the patterns in this book with princess seams, the front side pieces have a little bit of ease built into the seam between the two bust notches.*

1. Staystitch (see page 33) the center front piece along each curve of a princess seam ½ in/ 12 mm from the edge. Start stitching at the armhole edge and stop stitching after the curve, where the edge straightens out {fig. 25}. Repeat on the center back piece.

2. Pin the center and side pieces together at each notch, then at the armhole and bottom edge. Clip into the seam allowance along the curve, on the staystitched piece only, about every ¼ in/6 mm or so. Clip close to the staystitches, but don't cut through them. Continue to pin around the curves, pinning as much as

necessary along the curves to help evenly spread out the front ease. Be sure to pin the pieces together along the seam line and not along the raw edges {fig. 26}.

3. Sew the princess seams together with the staystitched or center piece on top. This will allow the feed dogs (the teeth under the presser foot) of your sewing machine to do most of the work easing the side piece in. Be sure that there are no puckers along the princess seams. Clip small V shapes into the side piece seam allowance, and press the seam open.

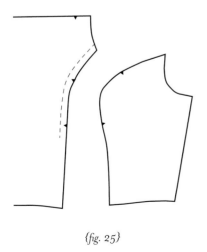

{fig. 25}

{fig. 26}

SEAM FINISHES

Seam finishing is necessary for any exposed raw edges on a garment. Raw edges that aren't exposed—such as the seams that join facings to a garment or the seams to join two collar pieces—don't require seam finishing. Seam finishes extend the life of your garment, prevent fraying, and neaten up the inside of your garment. There are many different types of seam finishes, and I will cover five different ones here. If you have a favorite method that I don't cover, feel free to use it where it is appropriate.

French Seam

This is a pretty way to clean-finish seams on sheer or thin fabrics. I don't, however, recommend using a French seam on bulky fabrics or on a tightly curved seam.

Sewing a French Seam

Note: *Most of the seam allowances in the book are ⅝ in/16 mm, so I used that allowance for this example.*

1. Sew the seam, wrong-sides together, using a ⅜-in/1-cm seam allowance *{fig. 27}*.

2. Press the seam open, then press it to one side. Trim the seam allowance to ⅛ in/3 mm *{fig. 28}*.

3. Fold the fabric along the seam, right-sides together, and press flat. Pin along the seam, then sew together with a ¼-in/6-mm seam allowance. The raw edge of the fabric is totally enclosed in this type of seam, making a smooth, neat garment interior *{fig. 29}*.

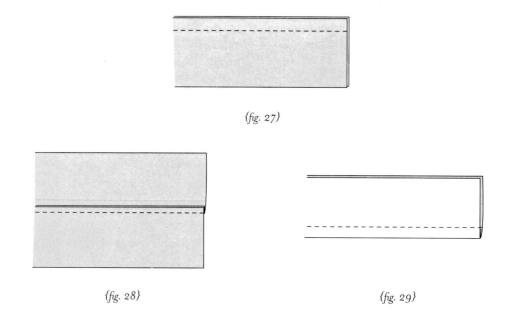

{fig. 27}

{fig. 28}

{fig. 29}

Hong Kong Seam

This is another pretty way to finish the seams on a garment. You can even do it in a contrasting fabric color if you want. A Hong Kong seam is best used on a stable fabric, and will add a little bulk to the seam edges. So if you want to use this seam finish on a bulky fabric, pick a lightweight fabric for the bias strips.

Sewing a Hong Kong Seam

1. Cut enough 1-in-/2.5-cm-wide bias strips to cover each side of the seam allowances. Piece together the bias strips if necessary (see page 12).

2. Sew the seam per the instructions and press the seam open. Fold all the layers away from one side of the seam allowance raw edge. Pin a bias strip to the seam allowance, right-sides together, and align the raw edges. Sew the bias strip in place with a ¼-in/6-mm seam allowance, catching only the bias strip and the raw edge of the seam allowance in the seam. Press the bias strip toward the raw edge {fig. 30}.

3. Wrap the bias strip around the raw edge, press, and pin in place. Edgestitch the inner folded edge of the bias strip, making sure to catch the folded-under bias strip in the edgestitch {fig. 31}.

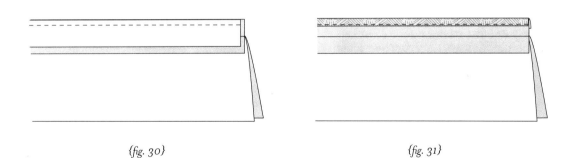

{fig. 30}   {fig. 31}

Pinked-Edge Seam

A pinked-edge seam finish is when the raw edges of the seam allowance are trimmed with pinking shears, which make a zigzag cutting edge that discourages fraying. This seam finishing is by far the easiest, but not necessarily the best for fabrics that fray easily or for use on a seam that gets a lot of stress or abrasion. It is a handy, quick way to finish seams if you plan to add a lining to the garment.

Sewing a Pinked-Edge Seam

1. Sew the seam per the instructions, press the seam open, then press it to one side.

2. Using pinking shears, or a pinking blade on a rotary cutter, trim off about ¼ in/6 mm from the seam allowance edges. Press the seam open again.

Serged-Edge Seam

When you run the raw edges of the seam allowance through a serger machine, the serger trims and finishes the raw edge, creating what is called a serged-edge seam. This is my go-to way to finish raw edges quickly and securely, but you do need to have a serger (overlock) machine to do this finish.

Sewing a Serged-Edge Seam

1. Sew the seam per the instructions and press the seam open.

2. Run each raw edge of the seam allowance through the serger separately, trimming off a tiny bit of the raw edge as you go. Make sure to only serge through the seam allowances.

Zigzag Seam

A zigzag seam finish is when you run the raw edges of the seam allowance through your sewing machine set to the zigzag stitch, which prevents the raw edges from fraying past the zigzag stitch. This finish can be used on many different types of fabrics. Zigzag close to the raw edge but not right along it, because the zigzag stitching can cause the fabric to buckle within the stitches, causing bulk.

Sewing a Zigzag Seam

1. Sew the seam per the instructions and press the seam open.

2. Set your machine to a wide, long zigzag stitch. Sew just inside each of the seam allowance raw edges separately.

STAYSTITCHING

Staystitching is used to add stability to areas that can stretch out if handled too much, like a neckline or an armhole. It is done immediately after cutting out the fabric pieces for a garment. To staystitch, using a normal stitch length, sew a line of stitching just inside the seam line on the seam allowance side. The staystitching line is retained, and it should be placed within the seam allowance but close to the actual seam line. When staystitching, always stitch in the same direction. On an armhole, start at the shoulder edge, stitch around the curve, and end at the side seam edge. Repeat this on each armhole. For a neckline, start at the center front or back neck and stitch toward one shoulder edge; then repeat on the opposite side of the neckline.

TOPSTITCHING

Topstitching is a line of stitching that is visible on the outside of a garment and is usually placed about ¼ in/6 mm from the edge, seam line, or fold. It is used to keep multiple layers flat, add strength to a seam, and as a decorative detail.

UNDERLINING

Underlining is a couture sewing technique that I love to use on all sorts of garments. It is a great way to add strength or stability to a lightweight or loosely woven fabric, gives you a place to hide your stitches if you don't want them seen from the outside of the garment, and in some cases can act as a lining if you don't want to line a garment. To underline a garment, cut out the pattern pieces from the underlining fabric first, before cutting out the garment pieces, and transfer all the pattern markings to the underlining fabric. Lay the cut-out underlining pieces on the wrong side of your fashion fabric, pin them, and use the underlining pieces as your pattern to cut out your fashion fabric. Then baste both the fashion fabric and underlining together just inside the seam lines within the seam allowance and along any dart legs. These basted-together pieces are now treated as a single layer and sewn accordingly. When choosing an underlining fabric, you want to match the weight of your fashion fabric as closely as possible and make sure that the underlining fabric can be laundered the same way as your fashion fabric. Some common fabrics used as underlinings are silk organza (very popular), organdy, batiste, muslin, and silk crepe.

UNDERSTITCHING

Understitching is a row of stitching that helps seams lie flat and keeps facings or linings from rolling to the outside of a garment. To understitch, press the seam allowance toward the facing or lining, grade the seam allowances (see page 17), then sew another row of stitching as close as you can to the seam on the seam allowance (or facing) side of the seam. Understitching is only visible on the inside of the garment.

ZIPPERS

Setting a zipper is an essential technique all dressmakers must learn. The procedure can scare off beginners, but just practice a couple of times and you'll master it. In the following, I go over two ways to set a zipper—a centered zipper and a lapped zipper. I use ¼ in/6 mm fusible web tape to "baste" a centered zipper in place, but you can just as easily substitute hand or machine basting instead of the tape.

Tip: If your garment will be washed, pretreat your zipper by putting it in the wash along with the garment fabric. Before sewing a zipper in a garment, I like to press the top ends of the zipper tape to the wrong side at a 45-degree angle. When sewing the zipper in place, make sure that the folded ends are caught in the stitching. This helps reduce the bulk of the seam allowance at the top ends of the zipper.

This type of zipper setting is usually used on the center back seam of a garment and creates two small "lips" of the same width on each side of the seam that cover the zipper.

1. Starting from the bottom edge, sew the center back seam together along the seam line; stop and backstitch at the zipper notch (where the bottom of the zipper will be, and the top of where the center back seam will be sewn together permanently). Don't remove the fabric from the sewing machine. Change the stitch length to the longest setting and baste the rest of the center back seam together. If there are any horizontal seams, like a waist seam, make sure they are matched up at the center back before continuing. Press the entire seam open and finish the raw seam edges with your preferred method.

2. With the right side of the back pieces facing up, carefully mark a line with chalk pencil and a ruler ¼ in/6 mm on either side of the basted center back seam, stopping at the zipper notch {fig. 32}.

3. With the zipper right-side up, place the fusible web along both zipper tape edges and finger-press in place. Unzip the zipper, remove the paper from the fusible tape, and place one side of the zipper tape, right-side down along the inside of the basted center back seam.

Make sure that the top of the zipper teeth are placed about ⅛ in/3 mm below the back neck seam line (or waist seam line, on a skirt) and that the zipper teeth are aligned along the center back seam. Close the zipper, then align the second side of the zipper tape in place. Once you are happy with the zipper placement, gently press with an iron along the zipper tape to fuse the zipper in place. Place the zipper foot on your sewing machine. If you don't have fusible tape, you can pin the zipper in place, then baste it to the seam allowance only, aligning the zipper in the same way you would with the fusible web tape. {fig. 33}

4. With the right side of the back pieces facing up, starting from the bottom of the zipper, topstitch (using a regular stitch length) along one chalk line, through all layers, to the top edge of the garment. Then stitch across the bottom of the zipper to the second chalk line, pivot, and topstitch through all layers along the second chalk line, back up to the top edge of the garment {fig. 34}.

5. Remove the basting stitches at the center back seam, and press.

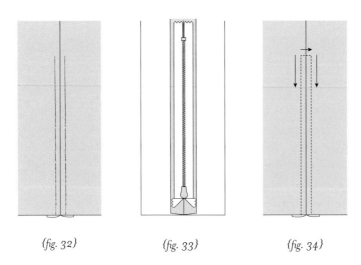

{fig. 32}   {fig. 33}   {fig. 34}

A lapped zipper is usually used at the side seam, but can be used at the center back if you prefer its appearance. Instead of creating two "lips" on each side of the zipper, like a centered zipper does, a lapped zipper creates only one "lip." The following instructions are for a lapped zipper being set into the garment on the wearer's left side seam, with the lip opening toward the back of the garment.

1. With the top edge of the garment closest to you and with the front piece on top, align the front and back along the right-hand (as you are looking at it) side seam raw edges and pin. Starting from the bottom edge, sew the right-hand side seam together as you would normally do; stop and backstitch at the zipper notch. Don't remove the fabric from the sewing machine, change the stitch length to the longest setting, and baste the rest of the side seam together. Press the entire seam open and finish the raw edges in your preferred method. Put the zipper foot on your machine.

2. Keeping the garment wrong-side up and the top edge closest to you, fold the garment fabric away from the back seam allowance. Place the opened zipper facedown on a single layer of the back seam allowance, making sure that the top of the zipper teeth are placed about ⅛ in/3 mm below the top edge seam line and that the zipper teeth are aligned along the side seam {fig. 35}. Pin the zipper in place and baste the zipper tape to the single layer of the seam allowance only, close to the zipper teeth.

3. Adjust the machine to a regular stitch length. Close the zipper, then flip the zipper over so the right side of the zipper faces up and all fabric layers are to the left of the zipper teeth. Edgestitch as close as you can to the zipper teeth, just to the right of the basted side seam {fig. 36}.

4. Lay the garment flat, right-side up, and the top of the garment closest to you. With chalk pencil, draw a straight line about ⅜ in/1 cm to the right of the basted side seam on the front piece, from the top edge of the garment to the bottom of the zipper. Then draw a short straight line across the bottom of the zipper. Pin all the layers together along the chalk line and carefully remove the basting from the top 4 in/10 cm of the side seam. Stitch the zipper in place, starting at the bottom short line, pivoting at the corner, and continue sewing along the chalk line toward the top edge of the garment. When you get close to the zipper head, put the needle down in the fabric, lift the presser foot, unzip the zipper a bit, drop the presser foot down, and continue to sew to the top edge of the garment. Remove the remaining basting stitches at the side seam {fig. 37}.

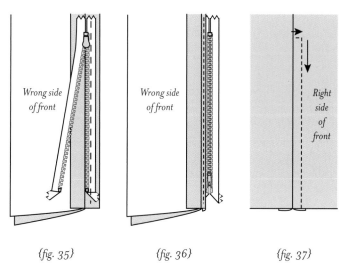

Wrong side of front

Wrong side of front

Right side of front

{fig. 35}   {fig. 36}   {fig. 37}

SIZING, PATTERNS, AND CUTTING

This section gives you the basics on sizing, tracing patterns, transferring pattern markings, cutting fabric, and making a muslin mock-up to test the fit of a garment. You'll also learn how to make pattern adjustments for the dress variation designs.

SIZING

The following sizing chart gives body measurements according to size. I wanted to include as many sizes as possible in this book, so I grouped the sizes into XS to XL, with a bigger jump in measurements between sizes than a typical home sewing pattern. This means that your measurements may fall between two sizes (I know mine do), but don't fret: when tracing off your pattern simply trace between the two sizes where your measurements fall. If your bust, waist, and hip sizes differ from the chart, draw a line on the pattern between the sizes to get the sizing you need.

	XS	S	M	L	XL
Bust	33 in 84 cm	36 in 91 cm	39 in 99 cm	42 in 107 cm	45 in 114 cm
Waist	25 in 63.5 cm	28 in 71 cm	31 in 79 cm	34 in 86 cm	37 in 94 cm
Hips	36 in 91 cm	39 in 99 cm	42 in 107 cm	45 in 114 cm	48 in 122 cm

The patterns in this book were drafted for a woman of average height (63 to 66 in/160 to 168 cm) with some curves and who wears a C-cup bra. If you are taller or shorter, then you might need to lengthen or shorten the patterns slightly. Always check fit by sewing a muslin mock-up (see page 38).

EASE

Ease is an extra amount built into a pattern to allow for body movement. The standard ease amount for the bust and hips is about 2 in/5 cm and for the waist is about 1 in/2.5 cm on a woven-fabric garment. I built ease into the patterns in the book as close to these standard amounts as possible. But for certain silhouettes, there may be slight variations, particularly at the waist. For the more fitted dresses with a waist seam—Joan, Ava, Audrey, and Grace—the waist ease is closer to ½ in/12 mm. For the dresses that don't have a waist seam—Mary, Diana, and Kate—the waist ease is more like 1½ to 2 in/4 to 5 cm. The knit garments tend to need less ease, since the fabrics stretch with the body. The exception to that rule is Anjelica, since the fit at the bust and waist is loose and the dress is meant to be belted with a low hip-slung belt.

Tip: The skirt pattern pieces of the Joan, Ava, Audrey, and Grace dresses are all interchangeable with the bodices. You can mix and match them to get a desired look.

TRACING A PATTERN

The pattern sheets provided in this book have printing on both sides of the sheets, so you will need to trace the pattern you want to use onto a new piece of paper. Any transparent paper will work for your traced patterns. If the paper you are using for tracing isn't large enough to fit the entire pattern piece, just tape pieces of paper together until you get the size you need. Remember to transfer all pattern markings (garment piece name, grainline, notches, darts, and how many to cut) onto your traced pattern.

CUTTING THE PATTERN OUT OF FABRIC

To cut out the fabric using your pattern pieces, refer to the layout diagram for each project, so you know how the pattern pieces best fit on the fabric. Sometimes you may need to flip a pattern piece to make it fit or cut out a pattern piece more than once; those issues will also be indicated in the layout diagram. Play close attention to the grainlines on the patterns and make sure to align the pattern pieces on the correct grain of the fabric. Once pattern pieces are laid out, pin them to the fabric layers (or weigh them down with heavy objects, if you prefer) and cut the fabric around the outline of your pattern, being as precise as you can.

Note: *Fabric yardage and layouts are for the most standard fabric widths available in the suggested fabrics for each project. There are many variables that would affect the necessary yardage for a project: if the fabric width is different, has a directional print, has a nap, or if you want to match a plaid or stripes. So calculate these variables when purchasing an amount of fabric for a project.*

TRANSFERRING PATTERN MARKS TO FABRIC

Transferring the pattern marks to the fabric is pretty simple and can be done in a few ways. I will discuss my favorite methods and what I find the easiest, but if you have a different method you like, feel free to use it. Keep the pattern pinned to the cut-out pieces. What marks should you transfer?

NOTCHES

The first marks I transfer are any notches. To transfer notches, just make a small cut in the seam allowance, about ¼ in/6 mm long at the center of the triangle notch on the pattern, making sure to clip through all pattern/fabric layers.

DARTS

To transfer darts, I use a tracing wheel and dressmaker's carbon paper. Remove any pins that may be in the way and slip the dressmaker's carbon between the pattern and the wrong side of the first layer (of two layers) of fabric. With the tracing wheel, trace along the dart legs and center fold of each dart. Then reposition the carbon paper so it is against the wrong side of the second layer of fabric and trace the dart again with the tracing wheel. The goal is to have all dart markings on the wrong side of each cut-out piece.

PIVOT DOTS

To transfer pivot dots, I make a small hole in the pattern where the dot is and transfer the dot to the wrong side of fabric with a chalk pencil or fabric marker. To transfer the dot to the wrong side of the second layer of fabric, push a pin through the dot marking, flip the cut piece over, and mark a dot with chalk pencil where the pin pokes through.

SEWING A MUSLIN

A muslin or toile mock-up is basically a test garment you make to see how a pattern sews up and fits you. A "muslin" is usually made out of muslin fabric in a similar weight as your fashion fabric, or a cheaper version of the fashion fabric. Muslins aren't finished garments; you just sew up the basic pieces of a pattern (bodice, sleeve, and skirt) to check the fit and overall proportions. I will admit that sometimes I cheat when making a muslin for a dress and only sew up the bodice, since that must fit correctly, knowing that I may need to make minor adjustments to the skirt after I cut it out in the fashion fabric. There are different opinions on whether to make a muslin; I am a true believer in making them, but the decision is all yours. I find muslins a valuable tool in getting the fit I want for a garment, before cutting into my more expensive fashion fabric.

MAKING A MUSLIN

1. Lay out all dress bodice and skirt pattern pieces on the muslin fabric and cut them out. If the dress has no waist seam, cut out the front and back pieces of the dress. Then transfer all pattern marks to the muslin fabric.

2. Follow the basic sewing instructions for the dress: staystitch around the neck and armholes, sew darts closed, sew the shoulders together, then sew all the vertical seams together (making sure to leave an opening where the zipper will go). There is no need to hem or attach facings, but I do press up the hem and press under the seam allowance at the neck and armholes.

3. Try on your muslin and take a look in a full-length mirror, to assess the fit. Do you see any pulling or any places with excess fabric? Do you like where the style lines or seams are hitting you? If you want to make any fit changes, pin or write on the muslin what you want to change, and go back to your pattern to make the adjustments.

FIT ADJUSTMENTS

Another whole book could be written about making fit adjustments, so it isn't a topic that I will discuss here. But see Resources at the back of the book for some of my favorite books on fit and making adjustments. You can also Google the fit adjustment that you need to make and see if there are any free online tutorials you can follow. For example, for the bust, there are two fairly simple fit adjustments you can make if you aren't a C-cup measurement: a small bust adjustment (or SBA) for an A or B cup, or a full bust adjustment (or FBA) for a cup size larger than a C.

PATTERN ADJUSTMENTS FOR THE DRESS VARIATIONS

All of the variations included in this book have some pattern adjustments that you will need to make to the original pattern. Please follow the red lines and text on each illustration to make the adjustments for the variations. A few of the patterns include variation lines that are labeled as such. All of the variation lines couldn't be shown on all of the patterns, since it would make trying to decipher which line to trace very difficult.

BEFORE YOU START

Before starting a project, be sure to review all the following bulleted points. This should be your cheat sheet before you make your first cut or stitch on any garment in the book.

- Read all instructions before starting a sewing project, and refer back to the Terms and Techniques section (page 11) for any instructions that may not be familiar to you.

- All seam allowances are ⅝ in/16 mm, unless otherwise mentioned in the instructions.

- All patterns and cut dimensions given include necessary seam allowances.

- Before cutting, pretreat all fabrics following manufacturer's care instructions and/or how the finished garment will be cared for. If you are going to only dry clean the finished garment, get the fabric dry cleaned first. And the same goes for hand or machine washing. There are many resources online with advice for pretreating specific fabrics.

- All seams are backstitched at the beginning and end of the seam. When basting by machine or by hand, do not backstitch.

- All sewing of knit garments is done with a narrow zigzag stitch (see page 23), unless otherwise mentioned in the instructions. If you own a serger machine, then all seams can be sewn together with that instead.

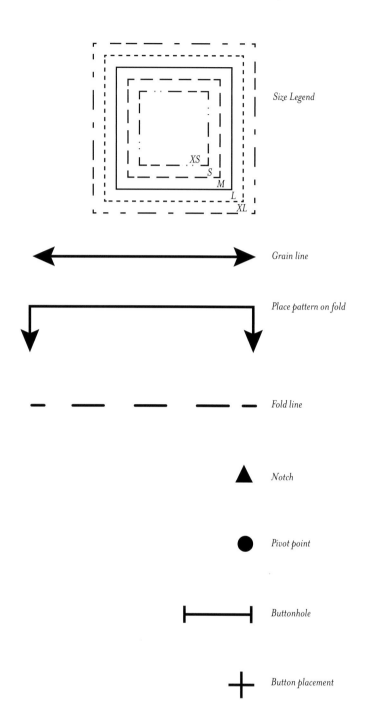

Size Legend

Grain line

Place pattern on fold

Fold line

Notch

Pivot point

Buttonhole

Button placement

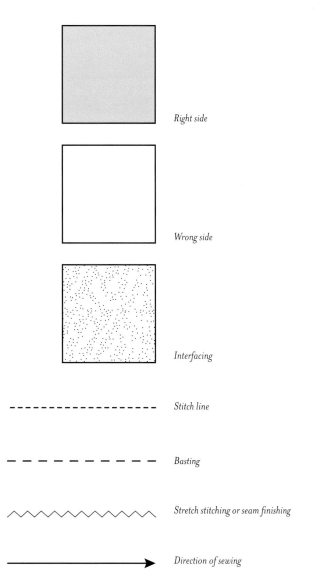

Right side

Wrong side

Interfacing

Stitch line

Basting

Stretch stitching or seam finishing

Direction of sewing

PART 2

THE FROCKS

COCO CHANEL

"Fashion fades, only style remains the same."–**COCO CHANEL**

Coco Chanel is synonymous with the Little Black Dress. She created and designed her first LBD in the 1920s and continued to design them throughout her career. Chanel was revolutionary in that she used jersey fabric to create her casual-chic dresses. Up to that point, jersey fabric was mainly used for men's underwear! Use of this fabric, combined with her simple silhouettes, was groundbreaking at a time when women were still wearing corsets. So it was only fitting to make this Chanel-inspired dress out of a beautiful wool jersey. This dress begs to be accessorized—go all out with lots of jewelry as Chanel herself would have done or keep things minimal with a simple scarf. And don't overthink it!

SUGGESTED FABRICS

Medium-weight wool blend or cotton blend jersey, rayon blend or polyester blend matte jersey, or polyester blend ITY (interlock twist yarn) jersey

TECHNIQUES

Sewing knit fabric seams (page 23)
Single-layer binding (page 24)
Hemming knit fabric (page 26)

MATERIALS

2¼ yd/2.1 m of main fabric (60 in/150 cm wide) for dress
⅓ yd/30 cm of clear elastic (⅜ in/1 cm wide) for shoulder seams
2 yd/1.8 m of satin ribbon (1½ in/4 cm wide) for belt and pocket trim
¼ yd/23 cm of satin ribbon (¼ in/6 mm wide) for belt loops
2 yd/1.8 m of fusible web tape (¼ in/6 mm wide) for hemming
Coordinating thread

TOOLS

Basic tools (page 10)
Ball-point or jersey sewing machine needle in size 70/10

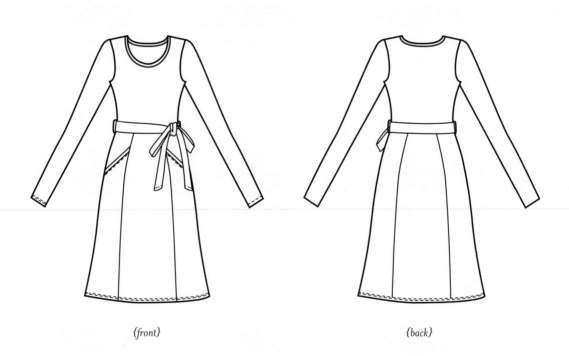

{front}   {back}

1. Trace the eight Chanel pattern pieces from the pattern in the front of the book, in your size. Cut out the traced pattern pieces.

2. Lay the pattern pieces on the fabric as shown in the fabric layout and cut out. Transfer all pattern markings to the fabric pieces after cutting.

3. Cut a strip of jersey on the cross-grain that is 1½ in/4 cm wide and 30 in/76 cm long for the neck binding.

4. Cut two pieces of clear elastic the same length as the shoulder seam on a Bodice pattern piece.

PATTERN PIECE LIST

Front Bodice (A)

Back Bodice (B)

Center Skirt (C)

Side Back Skirt (D)

Side Bottom Skirt (E)

Side Top Skirt (F)

Pocket Back (G)

Sleeve (H)

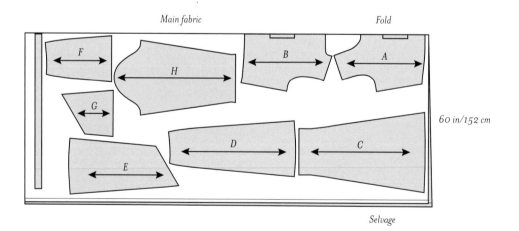

Main fabric

Fold

60 in/152 cm

Selvage

1. Sew the bodice.

a} Align the back bodice and the front bodice along the shoulder edges, right-sides together, with the front bodice on top. Lay one piece of the clear elastic along one shoulder of the front bodice ⅜ in/1 cm from the edge and pin all the layers together. Sew the shoulder seam with a double-stitched seam (see page 23), catching the clear elastic in the stitching {fig. 1}. Trim the seam allowance to ⅜ in/1 cm. With the right-side facing (so you don't melt the clear elastic), lightly press the seam allowance toward the back bodice. Leave the other shoulder seam open at this time; you will sew it when you bind the neck.

b} Finish the neck edge, following the instructions for single-layer binding on page 24. When you reach step 4 of the instructions, sew the second shoulder seam together as you did in step 1a above. The only difference is that you will need to also align the binding short ends together and sew the binding short ends and shoulder seam in one continuous seam.

c} Align the sleeve and bodice armhole raw edges, right-sides together, matching the sleeve notch to the shoulder seam, and pin together along the seam line. Be careful not to stretch either piece out of shape. Sew the sleeve to the bodice. Press the seam allowance toward the sleeve and trim the seam allowance to ⅜ in/1 cm. Repeat on the opposite armhole. Leave the side seams and underarm seams open for now.

2. Sew the skirt.

a} Measure the top slanted edge of the pocket back piece and cut two pieces of the 1½-in/4-cm ribbon for the pocket trim to that measurement. Press the ribbon in half lengthwise, wrong-sides together.

b} Align the long edges of the folded ribbon with the top slanted edge of the pocket back piece, and pin. Then baste them together ¼ in/6 mm from the edge. Flip over the pocket back piece (with the basted ribbon), align along the slanted edge of the side bottom skirt piece, right-sides together, and pin. The ribbon should be sandwiched between the two pieces. With the pocket back piece on top, sew the top edges together

{fig. 1}

with a ⅜-in/1-cm seam allowance. Flip the pocket back piece over along the top edge, so the ribbon is exposed and sewn pieces are wrong-sides together, and press flat along the ribbon seam. Edgestitch along the ribbon seam on the pocket side *{fig. 2}*. Repeat with the second set of pocket pieces.

c} Align the bottom edges of the side top skirt piece and the pocket back piece, right-sides together, and pin. Then sew together. Now there should be three pieces sewn together to make up the side front skirt. Fold the ribbon edge of the side bottom skirt up and align the ribbon seam with the notches on the side top skirt piece to create the pocket, and pin in place. Repeat with second set of side skirt pieces.

d} Align one edge of a center skirt piece to the center edge (the edge that has the pocket opening closest to the top) of a side skirt piece, right-sides together, and pin. Sew these edges together, press the seam allowance toward the center, and trim the seam allowance to ⅜ in/ 1 cm. Repeat on the opposite side of the center skirt piece with the second side skirt piece. This is now the front skirt.

e} Sew the side back skirt pieces to each side of the remaining center skirt piece, right-sides together. Press the seam allowances toward the center, and trim seam allowances to ⅜ in/1 cm. This is now the back skirt.

f} Align the front skirt to the front bodice along the waist edges, right-sides together, and pin. Sew the waist seam together with a double-stitched seam (like the shoulder seam), press the seam allowance toward the bodice, and trim the seam allowance to ⅜ in/1cm. Repeat with the back skirt and back bodice pieces.

3. Finishing.

a} Fold the bottom sleeve edge up ¾ in/2 cm, toward the wrong side of the fabric, and press to create a crease. Then unfold the sleeve edge.

b} Cut two 3-in-/7.5-cm-long pieces of the ¼-in/ 6-mm ribbon for the belt loops. Align the ends of the ribbon to the front side seam raw edges at the notches, and baste the ends in place ½ in/ 12 mm from the edge to create the belt loops *{fig. 3}*. Repeat on the opposite side seam.

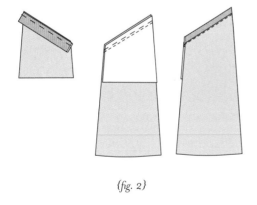

{fig. 2}

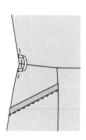

{fig. 3}

c} Align the side seam and underarm seam raw edges, right-sides together, and pin, making sure to match up the seams at the waist and underarm. Before sewing, make sure only the belt loop ends are caught in the side seam and that the loop is toward the center front. Sew the side seam in one continuous seam, starting from the bottom of the skirt and ending at the bottom of the sleeve. Repeat on the opposite side.

d} Fold the sleeve and skirt bottom edges under ¾ in/2 cm, to the wrong side, and hem (see page 26).

e} Try on your dress. Lace the remaining 1½-in-/ 4-cm-wide ribbon through the belt loops and tie in a bow. Cut the ribbon ends to the desired length plus 1 in/2.5 cm. Take the ribbon belt off, press the ends over ¼ in/6 mm to the wrong side, then fold and press the ends over again ¼ in/6 mm. Edgestitch along the inner folded edge of each end of the ribbon to hem and finish.

CHANEL VARIATION

The variation on the Chanel LBD has a more casual look. Reshaping the neckline and removing the sleeves and pockets creates a simple yet versatile dress that can be worn to work with a cardigan and flats or dressed up with some jewelry and heels for a dinner out.

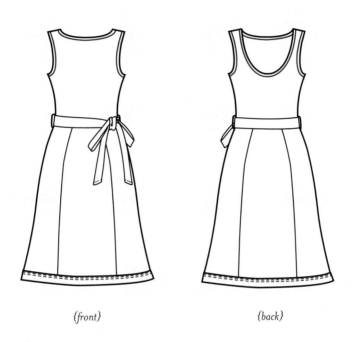

{front}   {back}

SUGGESTED FABRICS

Medium-weight wool blend or cotton blend jersey, rayon blend or polyester blend matte jersey, or polyester blend ITY (interlock twist yarn) jersey

MATERIALS

2 yd/1.8 m of main fabric (60 in/152 cm wide) for dress
⅓ yd/30 cm of clear elastic (⅜ in/1 cm wide) for shoulder seams
4 yd/3.7 m of ribbon (1½ in/4 cm wide) for belt and bottom trim
¼ yd/23 cm of ribbon (¼ in /6 mm wide) for belt loops
1½ yd/1.4 m of fusible web tape (½ in/12 mm wide)
Coordinating thread

TOOLS

Basic tools (page 10)
Ball-point or jersey sewing machine needle in size 70/10

1. Trace the following pieces of the Chanel pattern: Front Bodice, Back Bodice, Center Skirt, and Side Back Skirt (renamed Side Skirt for the variation).

   Note: *For the variation, you will need to cut 4 pieces from the Side Skirt pattern: 2 for the Back Skirt and 2 for the Front Skirt.*

2. Make the changes to the bodice pattern pieces, as shown in the illustration below and described as follows:

a} Raise the front neck 1 in/2.5 cm, then widen the front neck width 1 in/2.5 cm and draw the new neckline. Trim ½ in/12 mm evenly from the front armhole.

b} Drop the back neck 5 in/12 cm, then widen the back neck width 1 in/2.5 cm, and draw the new neckline. Trim ½ in/12 mm evenly from the back armhole.

3. Cut out the traced and altered pattern pieces. Lay the pattern pieces on the fabric as shown on the fabric layout, and cut out. Transfer all pattern markings to the fabric pieces after cutting.

4. Cut one 38-in-/97-cm-long strip of jersey on the cross-grain that is 1½ in/4 cm wide for the neck binding. Cut two 23-in/58-cm strips of jersey on the cross-grain that are each 1½ in/4 cm wide for the armhole binding.

PATTERN PIECE LIST

Center Skirt (C)   Altered Front Bodice (I)

Side Skirt (D)   Altered Back Bodice (J)

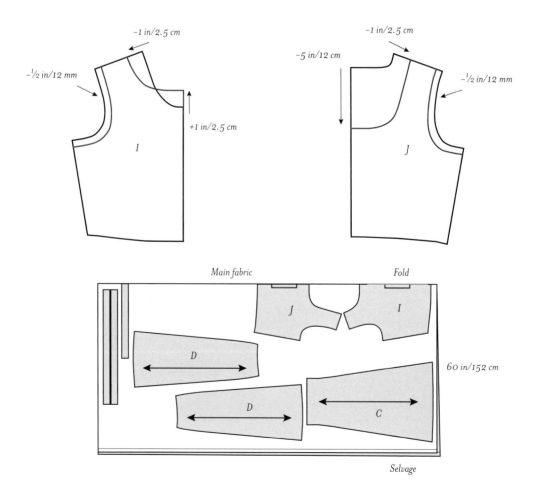

54

1. Sew the bodice.

a} Follow the Chanel instructions, step 1, omitting the sleeves. Finish the armholes following the instructions for single-layer binding (see page 24), stopping after step 3 of the binding instructions. The remaining steps for finishing the armholes will be done later.

2. Sew the skirt.

a} Skip to step 2e of the Chanel instructions, and do this step twice, once for the front skirt and once for the back skirt. Then work step 2f.

3. Finish the dress.

a} Skip step 3a of the Chanel instructions. Proceed to step 3b and follow the instructions.

b} Follow step 3c of the Chanel instructions, omitting reference to the sleeve. Instead, sew the short ends of the binding together at each armhole, as you are sewing up the side seams.

c} Finish the single-layer binding at each armhole per steps 5 and 6 on page 24.

d} Measure the bottom dress opening circumference and add 1 in/2.5 cm to that measurement, then cut a piece of the 1½-in/4-cm ribbon to that measurement. Sew the two short ends of the ribbon together with a ½-in/12-mm seam allowance to form a loop that is the same circumference as the dress opening. Press the seam open and finish the ribbon raw edges in your preferred method. Place the tacky side of the fusible web tape along one edge of the ribbon loop, on the wrong side. Remove the paper from the fusible web tape and finger-press the ribbon along the bottom opening of the dress, overlapping the edges the same width of the tape (½ in/12 mm), aligning the seam on the ribbon with one side seam of the dress. Then press with the iron to fuse the ribbon to the dress opening. Edgestitch along the top edge of the ribbon, then sew a second line of stitching ¼ in/6 mm below the first {fig. 4}.

e} Follow step 3e of the Chanel dress instructions to finish.

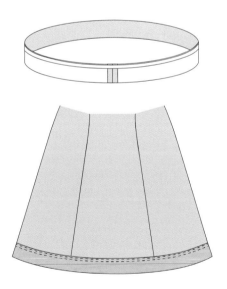

{fig. 4}

JOAN CRAWFORD

"I never go outside unless I look like Joan Crawford the movie star. If you want to see the girl next door, go next door."—**JOAN CRAWFORD**

At the beginning of her movie career in the mid-1920s, Joan Crawford was the quintessential flapper. Tired of playing flapper parts, she went on to develop a more sophisticated persona in the 1930s and earned true movie-star status. This 1932 photo of Joan proves that she and 1930s elegance were a perfect match. With her wavy hair and elegant, feminine dress, it is hard to picture her in the more masculine, highly tailored suits she preferred in the 1940s. The Joan dress draws on some of the pretty iconic details of the 1930s: a draped cowl neck, a bias-cut skirt, and—of course—a little bit of shimmer.

SUGGESTED FABRICS

Silk or polyester blend crepe-back satin (charmeuse), silk or rayon crepe, or rayon challis for dress body. The sequined fabric used for the overlay had a stretch-net base, but the stretch isn't necessary.

TECHNIQUES

Gathering (page 17)
Darts (page 15)
Sewing an all-in-one facing (page 16)
Centered zipper (page 34)
Baby hem (page 20)

MATERIALS

4¼ yd/3.9 m of main fabric (45 in/114 cm wide) *or* 3 yd/2.7 m of main fabric (60 in/152 cm wide) for dress
¼ yd/23 cm of sequined fabric (45 in/114 cm wide *or* 60 in/152 cm wide) for overlay
1 yd/1 m of lightweight interfacing (20 in/50 cm wide)
One 22-in/56-cm zipper and 1½ yd/1.4 m of fusible web tape (¼ in/6 mm wide)
Coordinating thread

TOOLS

Basic tools (page 10)

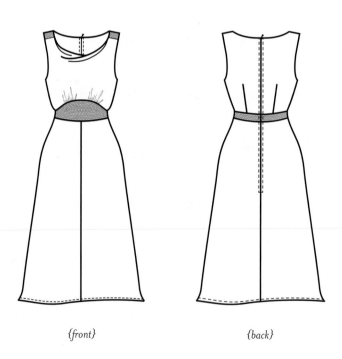

{front}   {back}

1. Trace the eight Joan pattern pieces from the pattern in the front of the book, in your size. Cut out the traced pattern pieces.

2. Lay the pattern pieces on the fabric as shown in the fabric layout and cut them out. Transfer all pattern markings to the fabric pieces after cutting.

PATTERN PIECE LIST

Front Bodice and Front Facing (A)

Back Bodice (B)

Front Waist (C)

Back Waist (D)

Front Skirt (E)

Back Skirt (F)

Back Facing (G)

Shoulder Overlay (H)

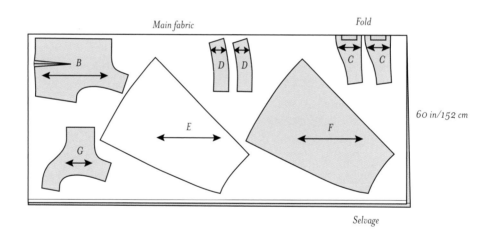

Main fabric

Fold

60 in/152 cm

Selvage

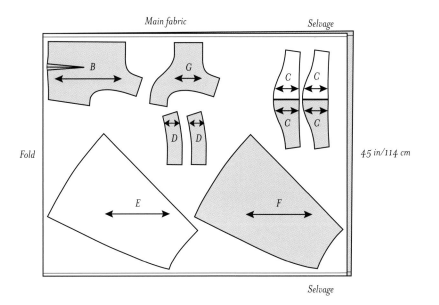

Main fabric   *Selvage*

B

G

C   C

C   C

D   D

E

F

Fold

45 in/114 cm

Selvage

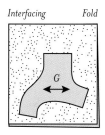

Sequin fabric   *Fold*

C

D

H

45 in/114 cm

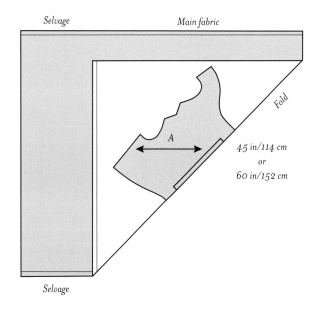

Selvage   *Main fabric*

Fold

A

*45 in/114 cm
or
60 in/152 cm*

Selvage

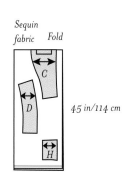

Interfacing   *Fold*

G

1. Prep the cut-out pieces.

a} Align the shoulder overlay piece and the back bodice piece at the notches, right-sides together. The opposite edge of the shoulder overlay should be pointing toward the waist. Pin the two pieces together between the notches. Sew the pieces together in a straight line between the notches, clip the shoulder overlay seam allowance to ¼ in/6 mm, and flip over so the sequin side is up. Align the pieces along the shoulder seam and baste together at the shoulder edge within the seam allowance *{fig. 1}*.

b} Keep the front bodice and the front waist pieces folded in half. Clip a small notch in the seam allowance at the bottom edge of the front bodice center front fold. Clip small notches in the seam allowance at the top and bottom edges of the front waist center front fold.

c} Staystitch the neckline and armholes of the back bodice and back facing pieces ½ in/12 mm from the edge. Staystitch the armholes of the front bodice (including those of the attached armhole facing) ½ in/12 mm from the edge.

d} Baste or fuse the interfacing to the wrong side of the back facing pieces.

e} Machine baste three rows of stitching between each set of bust notches along the bottom edge of the front bodice (see Gathering, page 17). Clip about ⅜ in/1 cm into the seam allowance at the shoulder/facing notch.

f} With right sides facing up on both pieces, align all edges of the sequined front waist with one dress-fabric front waist piece, and pin. Hand or machine baste these two pieces together within the seam allowance, and now treat these as a single piece. Repeat with the sequined back waist pieces and one set (mirror images) of the dress-fabric back waist pieces. The sequined waist pieces will be referred to as "front waist" and "back waist," while the second set of waist pieces will be referred to as "waist lining" pieces.

2. Sew the darts closed, attach the facings, and sew the shoulder seams.

a} Sew both darts closed (see page 15) on the back bodice pieces.

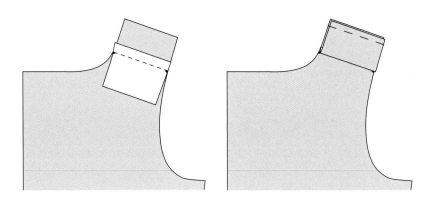

{fig. 1}

b} Fold and press the center back edges of the back facing pieces under, to the wrong side, ⅞ in/2 cm to create a crease, and then unfold.

c} Align one of the back facing and one of the back bodice pieces along the neck raw edges, right-sides together, and pin. Sew together, clip and grade the seam allowances, and press the seam allowance toward the facing. Then understitch (see page 33) the seam allowances to the back facing on the neck seam and press the facing to the inside of the neck. Repeat with the second back facing and back bodice pieces.

d} Align the back bodice (with the back facing unfolded) with the front bodice along the shoulder seam raw edges and pin. Sew the shoulder seams together at the bodice and the facings edges, then press the seams open. There's no need to finish these raw edges {fig. 2}.

e} Fold the shoulder seam in half and align the facings and bodice pieces at the armhole raw edges, right-sides together, and pin. Make sure that the back facing is aligned with the back bodice armhole and the front facing is aligned with the front bodice armhole. Sew together, then clip and grade the seam allowances. Turn the bodice right-side out and press as you would for an all-in-one facing (see page 16), leaving the side seams unsewn.

f} Finish the bottom edges of the back facing pieces and the front neck cowl raw edge by either pinking the edge or using a zigzag stitch. Then fold and press these edges under to the wrong side ¼ in/6 mm and edgestitch.

3. Sew the bodice side seams and attach the waist pieces to the bodice.

a} Flip the facings up at the side seam. Align the front facing and front bodice with the back facing and back bodice pieces along the side seam edges, right-sides together, and pin. Make sure the armhole seam is matched up. Sew the side seams together in one continuous seam from the facing edge to the bottom edge of the bodice, then press open (see Sewing an All-in-One Facing, step 4). Finish the raw edges with your preferred method. Turn the facing to the inside of the bodice.

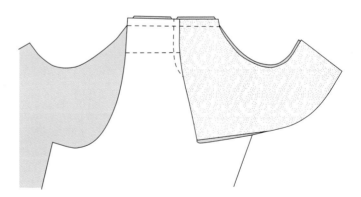

{fig. 2}

b} Align the front waist and back waist pieces along the side seam raw edges and pin. Sew together and lightly press open, being careful not to melt the sequins in the seam allowance with the hot iron. Repeat with the waist lining pieces.

c} Gather the front bodice between each set of bust notches to measure approximately the width between the corresponding notches on the front waist piece by gently pulling the bobbin threads of the basting stitches. Align the bottom of the joined bodice and top of the joined waist pieces along the raw edges and pin, making sure to distribute the bust gathers evenly and to match notches and side seams. Baste the pieces together ½ in/12 mm from the raw edge.

d} Place the right side of the waist lining piece on top of the wrong side of the bodice, align the raw edges as in step 3c (the bodice should be sandwiched between the waist and waist lining pieces), and pin. Sew all the layers together, clip the seam allowance at the curves, fold the waist pieces away from the bodice, and gently press the seam allowance toward the waist seam.

e} Baste the bottom raw edges of the waist and the waist lining pieces together, and treat as one layer.

4. Sew the skirt pieces and join them to the waist.

a} Align the front skirt pieces along the center front seam, right-sides together, and pin. Sew together, press the seam open, and finish the raw edges in your preferred method.

b} Align the joined front skirt and one back skirt piece along the side seam raw edges, right-sides together, and pin. Sew together, press the seam open, and finish the raw edges in your preferred method. Repeat with the second back skirt piece on the opposite side seam of the front skirt.

c} Align the joined skirt piece with the waist piece along the raw edges, right-sides together, matching them at the side seams, and pin. Sew together and press the seam allowance toward the skirt piece. Finish the raw edges in your preferred method.

5. Sew the center back, insert a centered zipper, and finish the dress.

a} Flip up the back facing so it isn't caught in the center back or zipper stitching, and don't sew or baste the center back facing seam together. Align the center back seam raw edges, right-sides together, and pin. Make sure the waist seams match. Follow the instructions for a centered zipper on page 34. Make sure the top of the zipper teeth are about ⅛ in/3 mm below the neck seam line.

b} Hand tack the facing to the dress at the side seams with a few small backstitches. Only stitch through the seam allowance of the side seam of the dress, so the tacking doesn't show through to the outside of the garment.

c} Fold the center back facing edges under at the crease made in step 2b, and slipstitch the center back facing's folded edges to the zipper tape.

d} Since the skirt of this dress is cut on the bias, it is important that the dress hang for at least 24 hours before you hem it. After hanging, if the bottom edge of the skirt is uneven, straighten it by measuring down from the waist seam and trimming the skirt to the same length all around.

e} Hem the skirt by following the instructions for a baby hem on page 20.

JOAN VARIATION

The Joan variation is one of the four versatile separates included in the book. By removing the bodice and adding a simple facing at the waist, you end up with a very wearable A-line skirt. Make this skirt out of a solid fabric for a classic look or in a stripe for a playful basic.

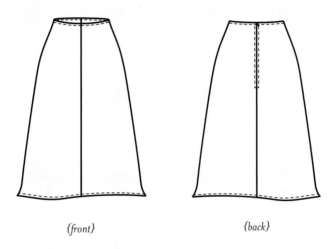

{front}   {back}

SUGGESTED FABRICS

Medium-weight twill, poplin, gabardine, or crepe—use a striped fabric to get the chevron effect
at the front and back seams

MATERIALS

2¼ yd/2.1 m of main fabric (45 in/114 cm wide) *or* 1¾ yd/1.6 m of main fabric (60 in/152 cm wide) for skirt
¾ yd/70 cm of interfacing (20 in/50 cm wide)
One 9-in/23-cm zipper and ¾ yd/70 cm of fusible web tape (¼ in/6 mm wide)
Coordinating thread

TOOLS

Basic tools (page 10)

1. Trace the following pieces of the Joan pattern in your size: Front Skirt and Back Skirt. Then trace the two Joan variation pattern pieces in your size: Front Waist Facing and Back Waist Facing. Cut out the traced pattern pieces.

2. Lay the pattern pieces on the fabric as shown in the fabric layout and cut them out. Transfer all pattern markings to the fabric pieces after cutting.

PATTERN PIECE LIST

Front Skirt (E)

Back Skirt (F)

Front Waist Facing (I)

Back Waist Facing (J)

Note: *The skirt shown is cut from striped fabric. Since the skirt is cut on the bias, the stripe will form a chevron at the center front and center back seams. So you will want the stripes to match up perfectly at these two seams. An easy way to do this is to use the grainline on the skirt pattern as the stripe match line. When you cut out the fabric pieces, make sure to align the grainline along one side of a stripe on the fabric for each piece cut. When laying out and cutting out to match stripes, you have to cut in a single layer, flipping over the Front Skirt and Back Skirt pattern pieces, for the left and right sides of the garment. The fabric layout for this project variation shows this arrangement.*

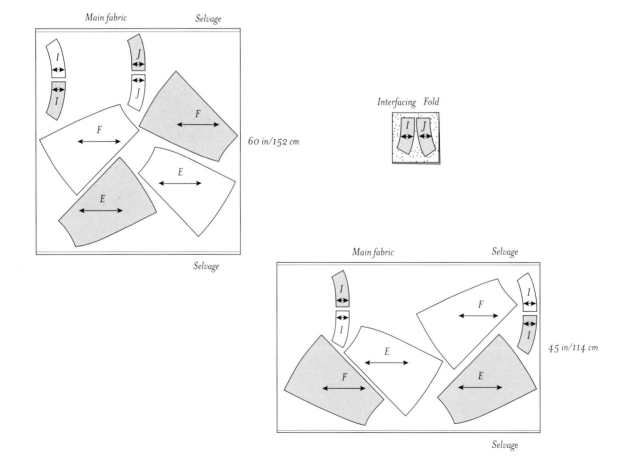

68

1. Prep the cut-out pieces.

a} Staystitch the waist edge of the front skirt and back skirt pieces, ½ in/12 mm from the raw edge.

b} Baste or fuse the interfacing to the wrong side of the waist facing pieces.

2. Sew the center front seam, and sew the center back seam and insert a centered zipper.

a} Align the front skirt pieces along the center front raw edges, right-sides together, and pin, making sure the stripes match all along the seam. Hand or machine baste the seam together, ⅝ in/16 mm from edge. Unfold the front skirt pieces and check that all the stripes are matched perfectly. If not, remove the basting, match up the stripes, and baste again. Once you are happy with the alignment of the stripes, sew the seam together. Press the seam open and finish the raw edges in your preferred method.

b} Repeat step 2a with the back skirt pieces, but only sew the center back seam together permanently from the bottom edge up to the notch and then backstitch. Then baste the rest of the center back seam together. Press the seam open and finish the raw edges of the seam in your preferred method.

c} Follow the instructions for a centered zipper on page 34, starting with step 2. Make sure that the top of the zipper teeth are about ¾ in/2 cm below the waist raw edge on the back skirt pieces. After sewing the waist seam, the teeth will be ⅛ in/3 mm from edge of the waist.

3. Sew the side seams and attach the waist facing.

a} Align the front and back pieces along the side seam edges, right-sides together, and pin. You'll notice that since the stripes are matched at the center front and center back seams, they may not match up at the side seams. Sew the side seams together and press open. Finish the raw edges in your preferred method.

b} Align the front waist facing and the back waist facing pieces along the side seam edges, right-sides together, and pin. Sew the side seams together and press open. There's no need to finish the side seam raw edges.

c} Finish the bottom raw edge of the joined facing pieces in your preferred method. Fold and press the center back facing edges under, to the wrong side, ⅞ in/2 cm to create a crease, and then unfold.

d} Align the skirt and facing pieces along the waist raw edges, right-sides together, and pin. Sew together, clip and grade the seam allowance, then press the seam allowance toward the skirt. Fold the facing to the inside of the skirt, wrong-sides together, and press the waist seam flat.

4. Finish the skirt.

a} Hand tack the facing to the skirt at the side seams with a few small backstitches. Only stitch through the seam allowances of the side seam, so the tacking doesn't show through to the outside of the garment.

b} Fold the center back facing edges under at the crease made in step 3c, and slipstitch the center back facing folded edges to the zipper tape.

c} Topstitch around the waist, ¼ in/6 mm from the edge, on the right side, starting and stopping the topstitching at the center back zipper stitching.

d} Follow step 5d of the Joan dress instructions.

e} Hem the skirt by following the instructions for a narrow clean-finish hem on page 21.

AVA GARDNER

*"I wish to live to 150 years old, but the day I die, I wish it to be with a cigarette in one hand
and a glass of whiskey in the other."*–**AVA GARDNER**

Ava Gardner exuded an inimitable, feminine sexy confidence. She was an intelligent and feisty woman who could swear and drink with the guys, and was quite the sex symbol in the 1940s and 1950s. Known as a femme fatale both on and off the screen, she never lost sight of her country roots. This dress is fun and flirty, with its knotted halter top and plunging sweetheart neckline. The 1947 photo of Ava captures the exuberance of postwar America, when fancy cocktail attire in luxurious fabrics was all the rage. (I don't think anyone has looked this good in a satin gown since!)

SUGGESTED FABRICS

Silk or polyester blend crepe-back satin (charmeuse), silk or rayon crepe, or rayon challis

TECHNIQUES

Gathering (page 17)
Centered zipper (page 34)
Baby hem (page 20)

MATERIALS

3⅝ yd/3.3 m of main fabric (45 in/114 cm wide) *or* 2¾ yd/2.5 m of main fabric (60 in/152 cm wide) for dress
¾ yd/70 cm of lightweight interfacing (20 in/50 cm wide)
One 14-in/35.5-cm zipper and 1 yd/1 m of fusible web tape (¼ in/6 mm wide)
Coordinating thread

TOOLS

Basic tools (page 10)

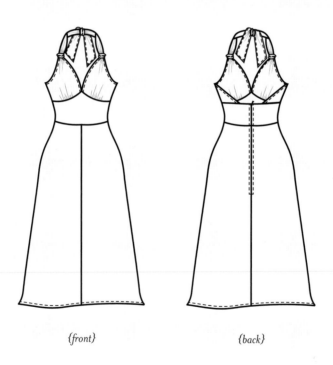

{front}   {back}

1. Trace the three Ava pattern pieces (Front Bodice, Front Waist, Back Waist) and the Joan Front Skirt and Back Skirt pieces from the patterns in the front of the book, in your size. Cut out the traced pattern pieces.

2. Lay the pattern pieces on the fabric as shown in the fabric layout and cut them out. Transfer all pattern markings to the fabric pieces after cutting.

PATTERN PIECE LIST

Front Bodice (A)

Front Waist (B)

Back Waist (C)

Front Skirt (E)
(from Joan pattern)

Back Skirt (F)
(from Joan pattern)

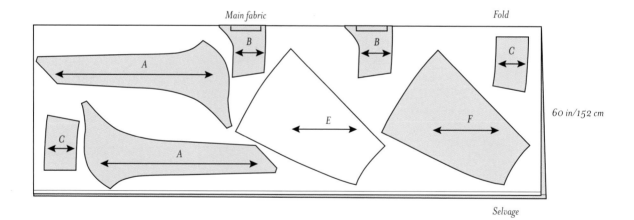

Main fabric

Fold

60 in/152 cm

Selvage

1. Prep the cut-out pieces.

a} Staystitch the neck and armhole edges of all bodice pieces ½ in/12 mm from the edge.

b} Baste or fuse the interfacing to the wrong side of one front waist and one set (mirror images) of back waist pieces. The noninterfaced waist pieces will now be referred to as the "waist lining" pieces. Fold the front waist and front waist lining pieces in half, and clip a small notch into the seam allowance of the waist edge along the center front fold.

2. Sew the bodice pieces and the waist pieces together.

a} Align all edges of two of the bodice pieces, right-sides together, and pin along the neck, armhole, and tie the raw edges. Sew together the neck, armhole, and tie edges, pivoting at the tie ends. Grade the seam allowances, clip off excess seam allowance at the corners of the tie ends, and clip the seam allowance

around the curves (see page 14). Turn the bodice right-side out, gently pushing out the corners with a point turner, and press flat along the seams. With the right side facing up, edgestitch along the three sides that were just sewn together. Repeat with the remaining two bodice pieces. You now have two fully lined bodice pieces that are mirror images.

b} Align the bottom raw edges of one bodice piece and machine baste three rows of stitching between the two bust notches (see the instructions for gathering, page 17). Repeat for the second bodice piece.

c} Align the front waist and one back waist piece along the side seam raw edges, right-sides together, and pin. Sew together and press the seam open; there's no need to finish these raw edges. Repeat on the opposite side of the front waist with the second back waist piece. Then repeat this entire step with the front and

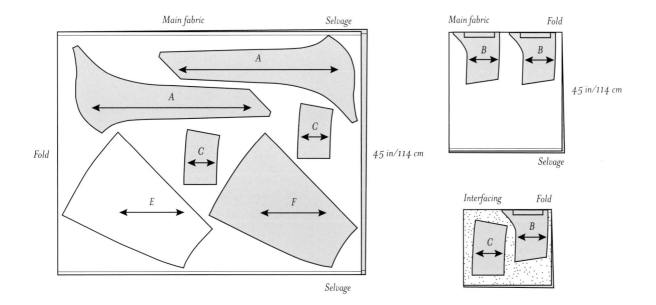

back waist lining pieces. Fold and press the center back waist lining edges under, to the wrong side, ⅞ in/2 cm, to create a crease, then unfold. Fold and press the bottom edge of the waist lining under, to the wrong side, ⅝ in/16 mm, to create a crease, then unfold.

d} Gather both bodice pieces (between each set of bust notches) to approximately the width of the corresponding notches on the front waist piece, by gently pulling the bobbin threads of the basting stitches. Align the bottom of each bodice piece to the top of the joined waist pieces along the raw edges, right-sides together, and pin. Make sure to distribute the bust gathers evenly, matching the bust notches and the notch on the bodice to the side seams of the waist pieces. The center front bodice edges will sit about ⅝ in/16 mm below the tip of the center front waist point. Starting at each side of the center front and working toward the center back, baste the pieces together ½ in/12 mm from the raw edge {fig. 1}.

e} Place the right side of the waist lining piece on top of the wrong side of the bodice pieces, aligning the raw edges, with the bodice sandwiched between the waist and waist lining

pieces, and pin. The bodice piece doesn't extend to the center back edge, so pin the two waist layers together where the bodice ends. Starting at each side of the center front and working toward the center back, sew all layers together. Make sure that each side of the center front bodice doesn't get caught in the stitching at the center front waist point. Trim down the seam allowance at the center front point, clip the seam allowance at the curves, fold the waist pieces away from the bodice, and gently press the seam allowance toward the waist pieces. Remove any visible basting stitches.

3. Sew the skirt pieces and join to the waist.

a} Align the front skirt pieces along the center front seam, right-sides together, and pin. Sew together, press the seam open, and finish the raw edges in your preferred method.

b} Align the front skirt and one back skirt piece along the side seam raw edges, right-sides together, and pin. Sew together, press the seam open, and finish the raw edges in your preferred method. Repeat with the second back skirt piece on the opposite side seam of the front skirt.

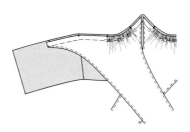

{fig. 1}

c} Align the joined skirt piece with the waist piece along the raw edges, right-sides together, matching at the side seams, and pin. Sew together and press the seam allowance toward the waist piece. The bottom edge of the waist lining is left loose on the inside of the garment for now.

4. Sew the center back seam, insert a centered zipper, and finish the dress.

a} Flip the waist lining up, so it isn't caught in the center back seam and the zipper stitching. Don't sew or baste the waist lining center back seam together. Align the center back raw edges, right-sides together, and pin. Make sure the waist seams match. Follow the instructions for a centered zipper on page 34. Make sure that the top of the zipper teeth are about ⅛ in/3 mm below the top waist seam line.

b} Fold the center back waist lining edges under at the crease made in step 2c, and slipstitch the center back waist lining folded edges to the zipper tape.

c} Fold the waist lining bottom raw edge under, along the crease made in step 2c, and slipstitch the waist lining to the waist seam allowance.

d} Since the skirt of this dress is cut on the bias, it is important that the dress hang for at least 24 hours before hemming. After hanging, if the bottom edge of the skirt is uneven, then straighten it out by measuring down from waist seam and trimming the skirt to the same length all around.

e} Hem the skirt by following the instructions for a baby hem on page 20.

f} Tie each side of the bodice into a loose knot, about 9 to 10 in/23 to 25 cm from the bodice/ waist seam. To get the correct placement of your knot, try the dress on and adjust each of the front bodice knots to a comfortable position above your bust and make sure the knots are even. If you like, you can hand tack the knots in place on the inside of the bodice. Tie the ends of the bodice ties into a knot behind your neck to create a halter.

AVA VARIATION

The Ava halter dress variation provides a bit more coverage. With the gathered skirt and a ribbon tie that laces through the front and ties around the back neck, it is the perfect dress for a summer party.

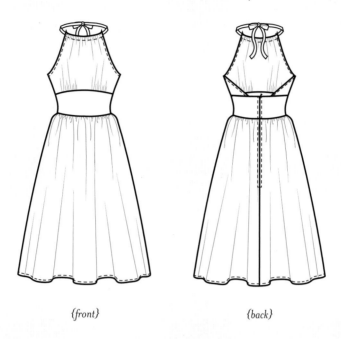

{front}   {back}

SUGGESTED FABRICS

Cotton voile, lawn, poplin, or lightweight linen for dress. Voile, lawn, or lightweight muslin for underlining and lining.

Note: *The dress pictured is entirely underlined with a solid cotton voile, so it isn't sheer; then the bodice and waist pieces are lined. If the fabric you choose is opaque, then you may not need to underline the dress, and in that case just line the bodice and waist pieces, ignoring any reference to underlining.*

ADDITIONAL TECHNIQUES

Underlining (page 33)

MATERIALS

2¼ yd/2.1 m of main fabric (45 in/114 cm wide) *or* 2 yd/1.8 m of main fabric (60 in/152 cm wide) for dress
2¼ yd/2.1 m of solid coordinating fabric (45 in/114 cm wide) *or* 2 yd/1.8 m of solid coordinating fabric (60 in/152 cm wide) for underlining (optional)
⅔ yd/60 cm of solid coordinating fabric (45 in/114 cm wide or 60 in/152 cm wide) for lining
¾ yd/70 cm of interfacing (20 in/50 cm wide)
1¼ yd/1.2 m of ribbon (⅝ in/16 mm wide)
One 14-in/35.5-cm zipper and ¾ yd/70 cm of fusible web tape (¼ in/6 mm wide)
Coordinating thread

TOOLS

Basic tools (page 10)
Safety pin

1. Trace these pattern pieces from the Ava pattern at the front of the book, in your size: Ava Back Waist, Ava Variation Front Waist. Then trace the Ava Variation Front Bodice. Draft one rectangle (onto pattern paper) in the following dimensions for the Skirt piece, in your size (see Skirt Piece Size Chart for sizing). Label this piece "Skirt, Cut 2 main fabric, Cut 2 underlining fabric," and place the grainline along the length of the piece.

2. Cut out the traced and drafted pattern pieces. Lay the pattern pieces on the fabric as shown in the fabric layout, and cut out the pieces. All the pattern pieces will then be cut out again in the underlining fabric (if using), then the bodice and waist pieces will be cut out again in the lining fabric. Transfer all pattern markings to the fabric pieces after cutting.

3. Take one set of the skirt pieces (main fabric and underlining), fold in half by aligning the short ends together, and cut each piece in half along the fold. These will now be referred to as the "back skirt" pieces.

SKIRT PIECE SIZE CHART

	XS	S	M	L	XL
Length	25 in	25¼ in	25½ in	25¾ in	26 in
	63.5 cm	64 cm	65 cm	65.5 cm	66 cm
Width	31½ in	34½ in	37½ in	40½ in	43½ in
	80 cm	88 cm	95 cm	103 cm	110 cm

PATTERN PIECE LIST

Back Waist (C)

Front Waist Variation (G)

Front Bodice Variation (H)

Skirt (I)

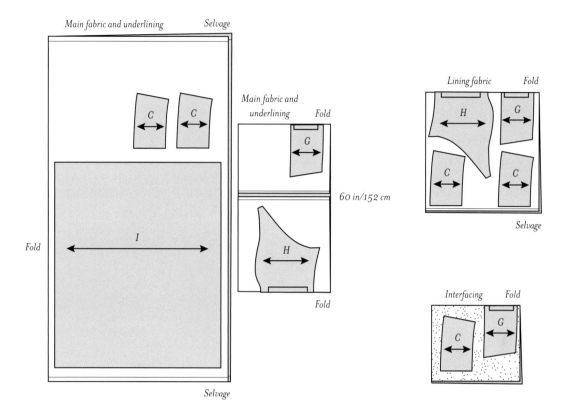

Main fabric and underlining · Selvage

C · C

Main fabric and underlining · Fold

G

60 in/152 cm

I

Fold

H

Fold

Selvage

Lining fabric · Fold

H · G

C · C

Selvage

Interfacing · Fold

C · G

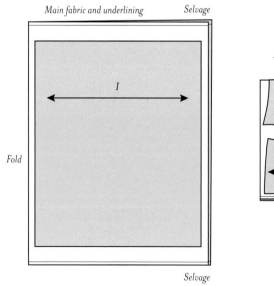

Main fabric and underlining · Selvage

I

Fold

Selvage

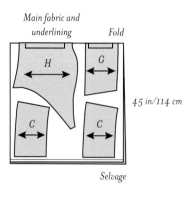

Main fabric and underlining · Fold

H · G

C · C

45 in/114 cm

Selvage

1. Prep the cut-out pieces.

a} Staystitch the armhole edges of the bodice lining pieces ½ in/12 mm from the edge.

b} Follow step 1b of the Ava dress instructions, but attach the interfacing to the wrong side of the front and back waist underlining pieces. Align all edges of the front and back waist pieces to the corresponding underlining pieces, wrong-sides together, and baste together ½ in/12 mm from the edge around the entire perimeter. Treat each of these basted-together waist pieces as one piece going forward.

c} Align all raw edges of the bodice and bodice underlining pieces, wrong-sides together, and baste the pieces together ½ in/12 mm from the edge around the entire perimeter. Treat this two-layer bodice piece as one piece going forward.

d} Align all raw edges of the front skirt to the front skirt underlining, and baste together along the side and top edges ½ in/12 mm from the edge, leaving the bottom edge open. Repeat on each set of the back skirt and back skirt underlining pieces. Treat each two-layer piece as one piece going forward.

2. Sew the bodice and waist pieces together.

a} Align all edges of the bodice and bodice lining, right-sides together, and pin along the armhole and top edges. Sew together, grade the seam allowances, and clip along the curves. Trim off excess seam allowance at the top corners. Turn the bodice right-side out and press flat along the seams. Edgestitch along both armhole edges.

b} Follow step 2b of the Ava dress, except note that there are two sets of bust notches on the single bodice piece, so each set will need basting stitches.

c} Follow step 2c of the Ava dress to sew the waist and waist lining pieces together.

d} Follow step 2d of the Ava dress, but you will only have one bodice piece that has two sets of gathers. The Ava variation waist piece isn't pointed at the center front, so you can baste the bodice to the waist piece in one continuous seam.

e} Follow step 2e of the Ava dress. The Ava variation waist piece isn't pointed at the center front, so you can sew the bodice to the waist piece in one continuous seam. Remove any visible basting stitches.

f} Make a casing for the ribbon to be laced through along the top edge of the bodice. Fold over the top edge ¾ in/2 cm to the wrong side, then edgestitch along the inner edge to form the casing.

3. Sew the skirt and join to the waist.

a} Align the front skirt and one back skirt piece along the side seam raw edge, right-sides together, and pin. Sew together, press the seam open, and finish the raw edges in your preferred method. Repeat with the second back skirt piece on the opposite side seam of the front skirt.

b} Machine baste three rows of stitching along the top raw edge of the skirt pieces (see instructions for gathering, page 17). Gather the top edge of the skirt to approximately the width of the waist piece by gently pulling the bobbin threads of the basting stitches.

c} Align the top edge of the skirt with the interfaced waist piece raw edge, right-sides together, and pin. Make sure to match the side seams and distribute the gathers evenly. Sew together, and press the seam allowance toward the waist piece. The bottom edge of the waist lining is left loose on the inside of the garment at this time.

4. Sew the center back, insert a centered zipper, and finish the dress.

a} Clip a notch into the center back skirt seam allowance, 8½ in/21.5 cm from the waist seam. Then follow steps 4a through 4c of the Ava dress instructions.

b} Make sure both layers of the skirt fabrics are even at the bottom; if necessary, trim to make both layers even. Then hem both layers as one, following the instructions for a narrow clean-finish hem on page 21.

c} Finish the raw edges of the ribbon. Press the ends over ¼ in/6 mm to the wrong side, then fold and press the ends over again ¼ in/6 mm. Edgestitch along the inner folded edge of each of the folded ends, to hem the ribbon ends. Attach the safety pin to one end of the ribbon and lace it through the casing. Remove the safety pin. Tie the ends of the ribbon into a knot behind your neck to create a halter.

AUDREY HEPBURN

"Elegance is the only beauty that never fades."–**AUDREY HEPBURN**

Audrey Hepburn and the LBD go hand in hand. Her most famous look was the gorgeous black Givenchy dress from *Breakfast at Tiffany's*, but my favorite Audrey frock is the full-skirted black dress from *Sabrina*. "The Sabrina Dress," as it would later be coined, was actually quite controversial at the time. Rumors abounded that Givenchy designed all the post-Paris costumes in the movie, while Edith Head took credit and even won an Oscar for the costumes. No one may know for certain who designed it, but either way the dress is truly iconic. This dress epitomizes one of the most popular silhouettes of the 1950s: a fitted bodice with a full skirt (often worn over crinolines) that emphasized a narrow waist. It's a classic yet elegant dress, much like Audrey herself!

SUGGESTED FABRICS

Silk or silk/poly blend dupioni, shantung, taffeta, or duchess satin for dress. Rayon Bemberg or china silk for lining.

TECHNIQUES

Princess seams (page 29)
How to line a dress (page 27)
Lapped zipper (page 35)
Baby hem (page 20)

MATERIALS

3 yd/2.75 m of main fabric (45 in/114 cm wide) *or* 2¼ yd/2.1 m of main fabric (60 in/152 cm wide) for dress
1 yd/1 m of fabric (45 in/114 cm wide) for lining
One 16-in/40.5-cm zipper
Coordinating thread
1¼ yd/1.2 m of satin ribbon (⅝ in/16 mm wide)

TOOLS

Basic tools (page 10)

Note: *The bodice of this dress is lined, to give structure and a finished look to the inside princess seams.*

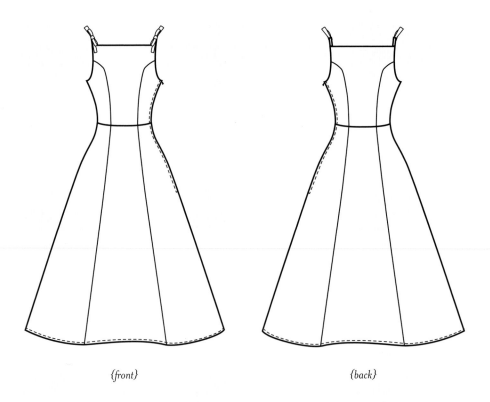

{front}   {back}

1. Trace the seven Audrey pattern pieces from the pattern in the front of the book, in your size. Cut out the traced pattern pieces.

2. Lay the pattern pieces on the fabric as shown in the fabric layout and cut them out. Transfer all pattern markings to the fabric pieces after cutting.

PATTERN PIECE LIST

Center Front (A)

Side Front (B)

Center Back (C)

Side Back (D)

Center Skirt (E)

Side Skirt (F)

Strap (G)

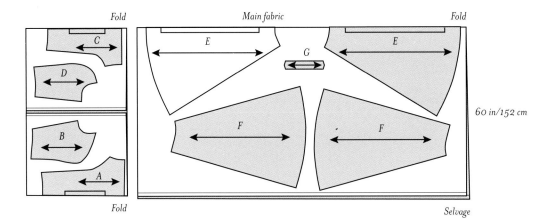

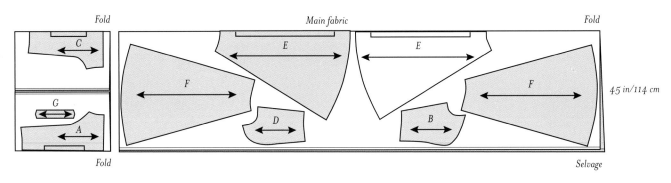

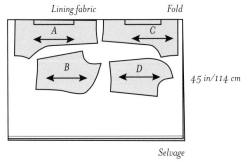

1. Prep the cut-out pieces.

a} Staystitch at the neckline and armholes of the center front and center back pieces ½ in/12 mm from the raw edge. Staystitch the armholes of the side front and side back pieces ½ in/12 mm from the raw edge. Repeat on the lining pieces.

b} Fold the strap pieces in half lengthwise, aligning the long raw edges, right-sides together, and pin. Sew the long edges together using a ¼-in/6-mm seam allowance, then turn the strap right-side out through one of the open ends. Press the strap flat along the seam.

2. Sew the bodice and lining together.

a} Follow the instructions for a princess seam on page 29 to join the center front and side front pieces together. Repeat on the front lining pieces.

b} Repeat step 2a on the back and back lining pieces; the back pieces don't have any ease added to the princess seam.

c} With the front bodice right-side up, align the strap ends along the top edge of the front bodice, place the seamed side of the strap just inside the notch, and pin in place. Baste the straps to the front bodice ½ in/12 mm from the edge. Then align the opposite strap ends along the top edge of the back bodice and repeat the preceding instruction for the front bodice. The two bodice pieces are joined by two strap pieces {fig. 1}. Now would be a good time to slip the bodice over your head and check that the strap length is correct. Make adjustments if necessary.

d} Fold over and press the bottom edges of the lining to the wrong side ⅝ in/16 mm, then unfold, leaving a pressed crease. With the wrong side of the front lining facing up, fold over and press to the wrong side 1 in/2.5 cm on the right-hand side seam of the piece (this will be the left side seam on the finished garment). With the wrong side of the back lining

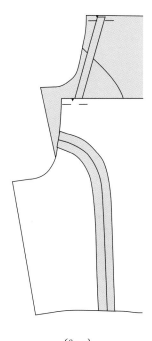

{fig. 1}

facing up, fold over and press ¾ in/2 cm at the left-hand side of the piece (left side seam) to the wrong side. Unfold the pressed edges of the lining, leaving a crease.

e} Align the front bodice with the front lining along the armholes and the top raw edges, right-sides together, with the straps sandwiched between, and pin. Sew together along the armholes and top edge, pivot around the corners, and make sure not to catch the straps in the armhole stitching (you only want the straps caught in the top edge) {fig. 2}. The side seams are left unsewn at this time. Grade the seam allowances, trim off the corners, and clip the seam allowances around the curves, being careful not to cut the stitching. Press the seam allowance along the top edge, between the straps, toward the lining. Understitch (see page 33) the top edge only between the straps. Turn right-side out and press flat along the armhole and top edge seams. Repeat with the back bodice and back lining, making sure the straps aren't twisted.

f} Flip the linings up at the side seams, so that the bottom edges of the linings are positioned above the armholes. With the wrong side of the front pieces facing up and waist edge closest to you, right-sides together, align the raw edges of the lining, front, and back bodice pieces along the right-hand side seam raw edges, and pin. Make sure that the armhole seams are matched up, then sew the entire side seam together and press the seam open (just like step 4 of sewing an all-in-one facing, page 16). Fold the lining to the inside of the bodice and press flat along the armhole seam. Leave the wearer's left side seam unsewn at this point.

3. Sew the skirt pieces together and attach the skirt to the bodice.

a} Align one center skirt piece with one side skirt piece along the long raw edge, right-sides together, matching up the single notches, and pin. Sew together, press the seam open, and finish the raw edges in your preferred method. Repeat on the opposite side of the center skirt with another side skirt piece. Repeat the entire step with the remaining skirt pieces.

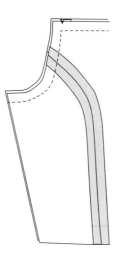

{fig. 2}

b} Align both joined skirt panels along the side seam raw edges, right-sides together. With the the bottom edge closest to you, pin together the right-hand side seam only. Sew together, press open, and finish the raw edges in your preferred method.

c} Align the skirt to the bodice along the waist seam raw edges, right-sides together, and pin. Make sure to match the princess seams and the side seam. Sew together, then press the seam allowance toward the bodice. Do not catch the waist edge of the lining; leave the lining waist edge loose inside the dress at this time.

4. Insert the lapped zipper and finish the dress.

a} Flip the lining up and out of the way, so it is not caught in the side seam or the zipper stitching, and don't sew or baste the lining side seam together. Follow the lapped zipper instructions on page 35. Make sure that the waist and armhole seams are matched up and that the top of the zipper teeth is about 1/8 in/3 mm below the armhole seam line. Fold the lining to the inside and press flat along the armhole seam.

b} Fold the wearer's left lining edges under at the crease made in step 2d, and slipstitch the lining folded edges to the zipper tape.

c} Fold the lining waist raw edge under along the crease made in step 2d, and slipstitch the lining to the waist seam allowance.

d} Hem the dress following the baby hem instructions on page 20.

e} Cut the satin ribbon in half and tie each piece into a bow, then tack into place on each strap with a few hidden backstitches. Cut off the ribbon ends at an angle so each one forms a shallow V shape to finish.

AUDREY VARIATION

The Audrey variation dress combines the bodice of the Audrey dress with the skirt of the Grace dress, creating a streamlined silhouette. This little number made in yellow linen is great for the office when paired with a cute jacket. For an elegant cocktail dress, make the dress out of silk shantung.

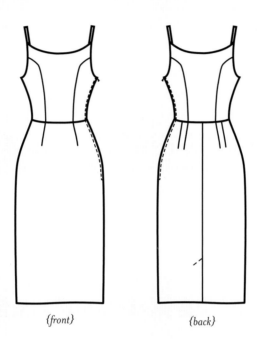

{front}   {back}

SUGGESTED FABRICS

Linen, cotton piqué, medium-weight cotton poplin, lightweight wool, or silk shantung for dress. Rayon Bemberg or china silk for lining.

ADDITIONAL TECHNIQUES

Blind hemming with seam binding or lace (page 21)

MATERIALS

1⅞ yd/1.7 m of main fabric (45 in/114 cm wide) or 1¼ yd/1.2 m of main fabric (60 in/152 cm wide) for dress
1 yd/1 m of fabric (45 in/114 cm wide) for lining
1½ yd/1.4 m of seam binding or lace trim (optional) for hem
One 16-in/40.5-cm zipper
Coordinating thread

TOOLS

Basic tools (page 10)

1. Trace the following pieces of the Audrey pattern: Center Front, Side Front, Center Back, Side Back, and Strap. Then trace the following pieces of the Grace pattern: Front Skirt and Back Skirt.

2. Make the changes to the Center Front and Center Back pattern pieces as shown in the illustration and described as follows:

a} Drop the Center Front neck 1¼ in/3 cm and draw a new front neckline, blending the line to be 1 in/2.5 cm from the strap notch. Repeat this step with the Center Back neck.

3. Cut out the traced and altered pattern pieces. Lay the pattern pieces on the fabric, as shown in the fabric layout, and cut them out. Transfer all pattern markings to the fabric pieces after cutting.

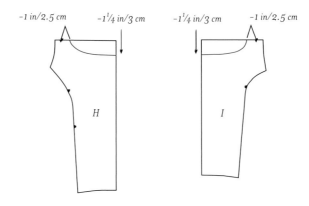

PATTERN PIECE LIST

Side Front (B)

Side Back (D)

Front Skirt (E)
(from Grace pattern)

Back Skirt (F)
(from Grace pattern)

Strap (G)

Altered Center Front (H)

Altered Center Back (I)

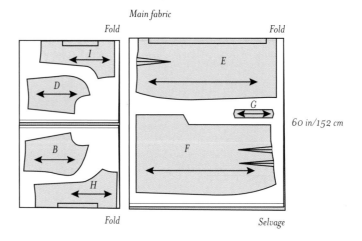

1. Prep the cut-out pieces.

a} Follow steps 1a and 1b of the Audrey dress sewing instructions.

2. Sew the bodice and lining together.

a} Follow steps 2a through 2f of the Audrey dress sewing instructions.

3. Sew the skirt pieces together and attach the skirt to the bodice.

a} Follow steps 4a through 4d of the Grace dress instructions.

b} Follow steps 3b and 3c of the Audrey dress instructions, except make sure to match the front and back princess seams of the bodice with the front darts and inner back darts on the skirt.

4. Insert a lapped zipper and finish the dress.

a} Follow steps 4a through 4c of the Audrey dress instructions.

b} Finger-press the hem under to the wrong side 1½ in/4 cm, and pin in place. Try on the dress to confirm that you like the length and that the hem is even. Make any hem adjustments that may be necessary, then press the hem in place with an iron.

c} Hem the dress following the instructions for a blind hem with seam binding or lace on page 21.

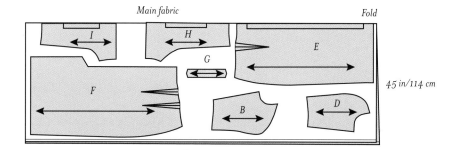

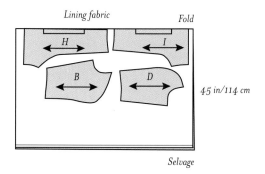

GRACE KELLY

"I don't want to dress up a picture with just my face."–**GRACE KELLY**

Grace Kelly embodied sophistication and understated style. She had poise beyond her years, retiring from Hollywood at the age of twenty-six to marry a royal ruler and fulfill her duties as Princess of Monaco. The black dress she wore in *Rear Window* is unforgettable, with its sheer upper bodice and portrait neckline. Originally designed by Edith Head, this dress is a bit more subdued than the average looks of the 1950s, and that's what makes it so special—you have to look closely at the details to fully appreciate it. My interpretation of the dress has a narrow pencil skirt rather than the fuller skirt of the original. Also, the original dress had sheer pleated fabric over the bodice and skirt. This sort of treatment and fabric is difficult to find these days, so I opted for a wool-blend ottoman suiting fabric that has a subtle stripe texture to mimic the pleated look. If you prefer a fuller skirt, feel free to substitute the A-line skirt of the Joan dress or go a lot fuller and use the skirt from the Audrey dress.

SUGGESTED FABRICS

Medium-weight wool suiting, wool gabardine, or wool crepe for bodice and skirt. Sheer fabric with body such as silk organza for yoke and collar. Rayon Bemberg or china silk for lining.

TECHNIQUES

French seam (page 30)
Narrow clean-finish hem (page 21)
Princess seams (page 29)
How to line a dress (page 27)
Darts (page 15)
Lapped zipper (page 35)
Blind hemming with seam binding or lace (page 21)

MATERIALS

1⅝ yd/1.5 m of main fabric (45 in/114 cm wide) *or* 1¼ yd/1.2 m of main fabric (60 in/152 cm wide) for dress
¾ yd/70 cm of sheer fabric (45 in/114 cm wide) for yoke and collar
¾ yd/70 cm of fabric (45 in/114 cm wide) for lining
1½ yd/1.4 m of seam binding or lace trim
One 16-in/40.5-cm zipper
Coordinating thread

TOOLS

Basic tools (page 10)

{front}   {back}

1. Trace all nine Grace pattern pieces from the pattern sheet in the front of the book, in your size. Cut out the traced pattern pieces.

2. Lay the Grace pattern pieces on the fabric as shown in the fabric layout, and cut out. Transfer all pattern markings to the fabric pieces after cutting.

PATTERN PIECE LIST

Center Front Bodice (A)

Side Front Bodice (B)

Center Back Bodice (C)

Side Back Bodice (D)

Front Skirt (E)

Back Skirt (F)

Front Yoke (G)

Back Yoke (H)

Collar (I)

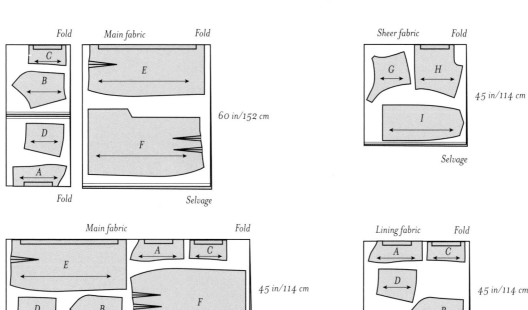

1. Prep the cut-out pieces.

a} Staystitch the neckline of the front and back yoke pieces ½ in/12 mm from the raw edge.

2. Sew the collar and yoke.

a} Align the center back straight edge of both collar pieces and pin. Sew together along the center back seam, trim the seam allowance to about ¼ in/6 mm, and press the seam open.

b} Fold the collar in half lengthwise; align along the short ends and the long curved edge, right-sides together. Lightly press along the fold, then fold over one curved edge ⅝ in/16 mm, wrong-sides together, and press. Sew each of the short ends together, keeping the pressed long edge folded up. Trim the seam allowance to about ¼ in/6 mm, and clip excess seam allowance off at the corner. Turn the collar right-side out, and press flat {fig. 1}.

c} Align the front and back yoke pieces along the shoulder edges, wrong-sides together, and pin. Sew both shoulder seams following the instructions for a French seam on page 30. Press the shoulder seams toward the back.

d} Align the right side of the long collar edge (not the folded-under edge) to the wrong side of the joined yoke neckline and pin. Sew the collar to the yoke, grade the seam allowance, and press

the seam allowance toward the collar. Then pin the folded long edge of the collar along the right side of the yoke, covering the neckline stitching just made. Edgestitch the collar folded edge to the yoke.

e} Hem the armhole edges of the yoke with a narrow clean-finish hem (see page 21).

3. Sew the bodice and bodice lining and attach to the yoke.

a} Follow the princess seam instructions on page 29 to join the center front bodice and side front bodice pieces together. Repeat on the front lining pieces.

b} Repeat step 3a on the back bodice and back lining pieces; the back pieces don't have any ease added to the princess seam.

c} Fold over and press the bottom lining edge to the wrong side ⅝ in/16 mm, then unfold, leaving a pressed crease. With the wrong side of the front lining facing up, fold over and press the right-hand side seam allowance to the wrong side 1 in/2.5 cm. With the wrong side of back lining facing up, fold over and press the left-hand side seam allowance to the wrong side ¾ in/2 cm. Unfold the lining side edges, leaving a pressed crease.

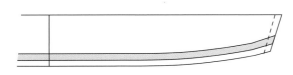

{fig. 1}

d} Align the bottom edge of the back yoke to the top edge of the back bodice, right-sides together. Place the hemmed armhole edges at the notches on each side back bodice piece and pin the raw edges together between the notches, making sure that the princess seams on the bodice align with the notches on the back yoke. Baste the seam together ½ in/12 mm from the edge. Align the right side of the back lining piece over the basted seam, sandwiching the yoke between the back bodice and the back lining, then pin in place. Sew all the layers together, from one side to the other. Grade the seam allowances, press the seam allowances toward the lining, and understitch (see page 33). Fold the lining to the inside and press seam flat {fig. 2}.

e} Repeat step 3d with the front bodice, front yoke, and front lining pieces. The only difference is that the front yoke is two pieces; each of the front yoke pieces will meet at the center front of the front bodice.

f} Flip the linings up at the side seams, so the bottom edges of the linings are positioned above the armholes with the wrong side of the front pieces facing up and the waist edge closest to you. Align the lining, front bodice, and back bodice pieces only along the right-hand side seam raw edges, right-sides together, and pin. Making sure that the armhole seams are matched up, sew the right-hand side seam together and press it open (just like step 4 of sewing an all-in-one facing, page 16). Turn the lining to the inside of the bodice and leave the wearer's left side seam unsewn at this point.

4. Sew the skirt and join it to the bodice.

a} Sew the front and back darts (see page 15) closed on the skirt pieces.

b} Hem the back skirt kick pleat edges, following the instructions for a baby hem on page 20.

c} Align the back skirt pieces along the center back raw edges and the top kick pleat edge, right-sides together, and pin. Starting from the top edge, sew the center back seam together to the dot, pivot, and continue sewing the top edge of the kick pleat together. Make about a ½ in/12 mm clip into the seam allowance at the pivot point, press the center back seam allowance open above the clip, and press the top edge of the kick pleat seam allowance toward the waist. With the wrong side facing up, press the entire kick pleat to the right, which will

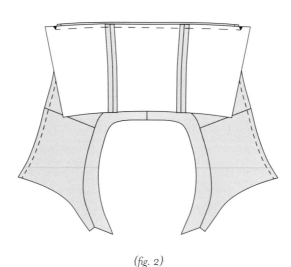

{fig. 2}

create the overlap and underlap of the pleat. Sew the kick pleat into place by stitching through all layers directly over the top edge seam of the kick pleat. On the right side of the skirt, the overlap will be folded under at the center back, the underlap will extend to the left side of the skirt, and there will be a diagonal line of stitching at the top of the pleat {fig. 3}. Finish the raw edges in your preferred method.

d} Align the back skirt and front skirt pieces with the front skirt on top and bottom edge closest to you, along the right-hand side seam raw edges, right-sides together, and pin. Sew the right-hand side seam together, press the seam open, and finish the raw edges in your preferred method.

e} With the bodice lining folded up and out of the way, align the joined skirt piece with the bodice piece along the raw edges, right-sides together, matching the bodice princess seams with the front darts and inside back darts of the skirt and at the right side seam, and pin. Sew the seam together and press the seam allowance toward the bodice piece. The bottom edge of the bodice lining is left loose on the inside of the garment at this time.

5. Insert a lapped zipper and finish the dress.

a} Flip the lining up, so it isn't caught in the side seam or zipper stitching, and don't sew or baste the lining side seam together. Follow the instructions for a lapped zipper on page 35. Make sure that the waist and armhole seams are matched up and that the top of the zipper teeth is about ⅛ in/3 mm below the armhole seam line.

b} Fold the wearer's left lining side seam edges under at the creases made in step 3c, and slipstitch the folded edges to the zipper tape.

c} Fold the lining waist raw edge under along the crease made in step 3c, and slipstitch the lining to the waist seam allowance.

d} Finger-press the hem under to the wrong side 1½ in/4 cm, and pin in place. Try on the dress to confirm that you like the length and that the hem is even. Make any hem adjustments that may be necessary, then press the hem in place.

e} Hem the dress, following the instructions for a blind hem with seam binding on page 21 to finish.

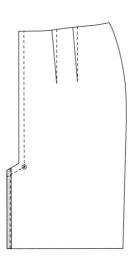

{fig. 3}

GRACE VARIATION

The Grace variation is a stylish, versatile, basic pencil skirt. This wardrobe staple can be made in many different fabrics, depending on your preference.

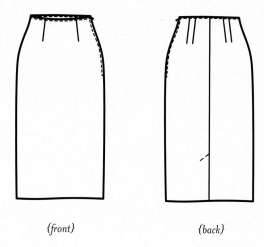

{front}   {back}

SUGGESTED FABRICS

Medium-weight suiting, gabardine, crepe, twill, or poplin

MATERIALS

1¾ yd/1.6 m of main fabric (45 in/114 cm wide) *or* 1¼ yd/1.2 m of main fabric (60 in/152 cm wide) for skirt
¾ yd/70 cm of interfacing (20 in/50 cm wide)
One 9-in/23-cm zipper
Coordinating thread

TOOLS

Basic tools (page 10)

1. Trace the following pieces of the Grace pattern, in your size: Front Skirt and Back Skirt. Then trace the two Grace variation pattern pieces, in your size: Front Waist Facing and Back Waist Facing.

2. Cut out the traced pattern pieces. Lay the pattern pieces on the fabric as shown in the variation fabric layout, and cut them out. Transfer all pattern markings to the fabric pieces after cutting.

PATTERN PIECE LIST

Front Skirt (E)

Back Skirt (F)

Front Waist Facing Variation (J)

Back Waist Facing Variation (K)

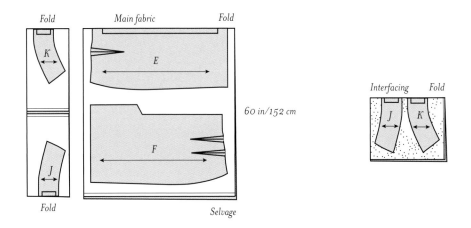

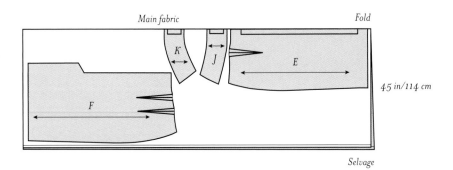

1. Prep the cut-out pieces.

a} Staystitch at the waist edge of the front skirt and back skirt pieces ½ in/12 mm from the raw edge.

b} Baste or fuse the interfacing to the wrong side of waist facing pieces.

2. Sew the skirt and facing pieces.

a} Follow steps 4a through 4d of the Grace dress instructions.

b} Align the front waist facing and back waist facing pieces with the back waist facing piece on top, along the right-hand side seam edge, right-sides together, and pin. Sew the right-hand side seam together and press open. There is no need to finish the facing side seam raw edges.

c} Finish the bottom raw edge of the joined facing pieces in your preferred method. With the facing wrong-side up, fold and press the seam allowance of the unsewn front facing edge under to the wrong side 1 in/2.5 cm. Then fold and press the seam allowance of the unsewn back facing edge under to the wrong side ¾ in/2 cm. Unfold the edges, leaving a pressed crease.

d} Align the skirt and facing pieces along the waist raw edges, matching at the side seam, right-sides together, and pin. Sew together and press the waist seam allowance toward the skirt. Fold the facing to the inside of the skirt, wrong-sides together, and press the waist seam flat.

3. Insert a lapped zipper and finish the skirt.

a} Flip the facing up so it isn't caught in the side seam or zipper stitching, and don't sew or baste the facing side seam together. Follow the instructions for a lapped zipper on page 35. Make sure that the waist seam is matched up and the top of the zipper teeth is about ⅛ in/ 3 mm below the waist seam line.

b} Hand tack the facing to the skirt at the wearer's right side seam with a few small backstitches. Only stitch through the seam allowance of the skirt's side seam, so the tacking doesn't show through to the outside of the garment.

c} Fold the left side seam facing edges under at the crease made in step 2c, and slipstitch the folded edges of the facing to the zipper tape.

d} Topstitch around the waist ¼ in/6 mm from edge, starting and stopping at the zipper stitching.

e} Follow steps 5d and 5e of the Grace dress instructions to hem and finish the skirt.

MARY QUANT

"The fashionable woman wears clothes. The clothes don't wear her."–**MARY QUANT**

The mini skirt, cute Peter Pan collar, and sheer sleeves on this dress will take you swingin' back to 1960s London. Inspired by the dress designed and worn by Mary Quant in this photo, this frock represents the mod style of her time. Mary Quant is actually known for coining the term "mini skirt" (named after her favorite car, the MINI Cooper). She was in the right place at the right time, designing clothes that she wanted to wear and that young women loved. In the '60s, women wanted more freedom in their lives, and that included clothing they could move around in. I gave this dress a bit more length to make it wearable for today. Feel free to shorten it if you want that true 1960s mini!

SUGGESTED FABRICS

Wool crepe, gabardine, suiting, or tweed for dress. Silk or polyester chiffon for sleeves. Silk or polyester satin, cotton poplin, or piqué for collar.

TECHNIQUES

Single-fold binding (page 12)
Darts (page 15)
Centered zipper (page 34)
Gathering (page 17)
French seam (page 30)
Buttonholes and buttons (page 14)
Blind hemming with seam binding or lace (page 21)

MATERIALS

2½ yd/2.3 m of main fabric (45 in/114 cm wide) or 1½ yd/1.4 m of main fabric (60 in/152 cm wide) for dress
¾ yd/70 cm of sheer fabric (45 in/114 cm wide or 60 in/152 cm wide) for sleeves
⅜ yd/35 cm of contrast fabric (45 in/114 cm wide or 60 in/152 cm wide) for collar
1 yd/1 m of lightweight interfacing (20 in/50 cm wide)
1¾ yd/1.6 m of seam binding or lace trim (optional)
One 22-in/56-cm zipper and 1½ yd/1.4 m of fusible web tape (¼ in/6 mm wide)
2 buttons ⅝ in/16 mm in diameter
Coordinating thread

TOOLS

Basic tools (page 10)

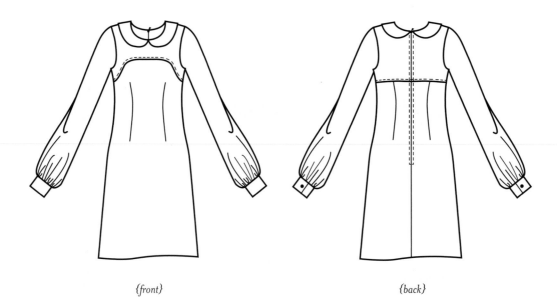

{front}   {back}

1. Trace the nine Mary pattern pieces from the pattern sheet in the front of the book, in your size. Cut out the traced pattern pieces.

2. Lay the pattern pieces on the fabric as shown in the fabric layout and cut out. Transfer all pattern markings to the fabric pieces after cutting.

3. Cut out two 9-in/23-cm strips of fabric on the bias, 1 in/2.5 cm wide, from the sheer fabric.

PATTERN PIECE LIST

Front (A)	Back Yoke (D)	Cuff (G)
Back (B)	Sleeve (E)	Front Neck Facing (H)
Front Yoke (C)	Collar (F)	Back Neck Facing (I)

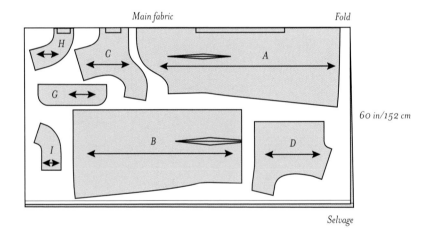

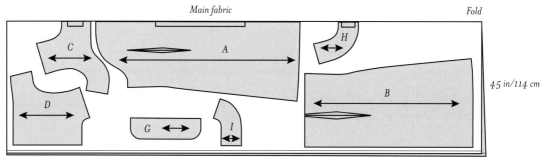

Main fabric

Fold

C

A

H

D

B

G

I

45 in/114 cm

Selvage

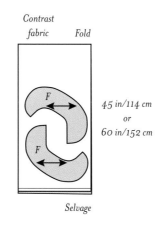

Sheer fabric

Fold

E

45 in/114 cm
or
60 in/152 cm

Selvage

Interfacing

Fold

I

H

G

F

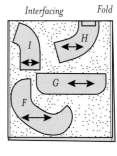

Contrast
fabric

Fold

F

F

45 in/114 cm
or
60 in/152 cm

Selvage

1. Prep the cut-out pieces.

a} Staystitch the neckline and armholes on the front yoke and back yoke pieces ½ in/12 mm from the edge. Staystitch the neckline of the neck facing pieces ½ in/12 mm from the edge.

b} Baste or fuse the interfacing to the wrong side of the neck facing pieces, to one set of collar pieces, and to one set of the cuff pieces. The set (mirror images) of collar pieces that has interfacing will now be referred to as the "top collar" and the set of collar pieces without the interfacing will be referred to as the "under collar."

c} Fold and press under the top straight edge on the noninterfaced cuff piece ⅝ in/16 mm to the wrong side.

d} Press each bias strip into double-fold binding, following the instructions for single-fold binding on page 12, and then pressing in half again lengthwise, aligning the folded edges.

2. Sew the darts closed and attach the yoke pieces.

a} Sew all darts closed (see page 15) on the back and front pieces.

b} Align the back yoke and back pieces along the yoke seam, right-sides together, and pin. Sew the pieces together, and press the seam toward the yoke piece. Finish the seam raw edges in your preferred method. These joined pieces will now be referred to as the "back." With the right side of the back piece facing up, topstitch along the yoke seam ¼ in/6 mm from the seam on the yoke side. Repeat with the second set of back yoke and back pieces.

c} Repeat step 2b for the front yoke and front pieces. The front yoke and front pieces have opposing curves; use as many pins as necessary and pin together at the seam line (not the raw edges). These joined pieces will now be referred to as the "front."

3. Sew the shoulder seams.

a} Align the front and back pieces along the shoulder edges, right-sides together, and pin. Sew each of the shoulders together and press them open. Finish the raw edges in your preferred method.

b} Align the front neck facing and the back neck facings along the shoulder edges, right-sides together, and pin. Sew the shoulders of the facing front and back together and press the seams open. Finish the raw edges in your preferred method.

c} Finish the bottom edge of the joined facing pieces in your preferred method. Fold and press the center back facing edges under to the wrong side ⅞ in/2 cm to create a crease, then unfold.

4. Sew the collar, and attach the collar to the dress with facing.

a} Align all raw edges of one top collar piece and one under collar piece, right-sides together, and pin along the outside curved edge. Sew together along the pinned edge, grade the seam allowances, and clip the seam allowance along the curve, being careful not to cut the stitching. Turn the collar piece right-side out, and press flat. Repeat with the second set of collar pieces.

b} Align the neck edges of the collar pieces, and machine baste the neck edges of the collar together ½ in/12 mm from edge. Repeat on the second set of collar pieces.

c} Pin the collar to the neck opening of the dress, with the under collar to the right side of the dress fabric. When you align the collar notches to the shoulder seams on the neck opening of the dress, the front ends of the collar should meet at the center front neck of the dress. Machine baste the collar in place ½ in/12 mm from the edge.

d} Align the facing neck edge to the dress neck edge, sandwiching the collar in between, right-sides together, and pin. Sew around the neck through all layers, starting and stopping at the center back edge. Grade the neck seam allowances and clip the seam allowance around the neck curve, being careful not to cut into the neck stitching.

e} Press all layers of the neck seam allowances toward the facing and understitch the seam allowance to the facing. Press the facing to the inside of the dress.

5. Sew the back pieces together, insert a centered zipper, and sew the side seams.

a} Flip the facing and collar up at the center back seam so they are not caught in the center back or zipper stitching, and don't sew or baste the center back facing seam together. Align the back pieces along the center back raw edges, right-sides together, and pin. Make sure the yoke seams match at the center back. Follow the instructions for a centered zipper on page 34. Make sure that the top of the zipper teeth is about ⅛ in/3 mm below the neck seam line.

b} Align the front and back pieces along the side seams, and pin. Sew the side seams together and press open. Finish the raw edges in your preferred method.

6. Sew the cuffs and the sleeves.

a} Align one interfaced cuff piece and one non-interfaced cuff piece along the curved edges, right-sides together, and pin; the straight edges of the cuff will not match up. Keeping the folded edge of the noninterfaced cuff piece folded over, sew together along the curved edge only. Grade the seam allowances and clip the seam allowance along the curve, being careful not to cut the seam stitching. Turn the cuff piece right-side out, and press flat. Repeat with the second set of cuff pieces.

b} Staystitch around the sleeve placket opening ⅛ in/3 mm from the sleeve placket slash line, then cut the sleeve along the slash line.

c} Fold the sleeve piece so that the entire sleeve placket slash forms one straight line. Take one piece of the double-fold binding, unfold, and pin one right-side edge of the double-fold binding to the wrong side of the sleeve placket slash, aligning the raw edges. Sew together along the first crease in the binding from the edge, and trim off about ⅛ in/3 mm of the seam allowance. Fold the binding over, encasing all raw edges, to the right side of the sleeve opening, and edgestitch the binding in place along the inner folded edge. Trim off any excess binding so that all raw edges are even {fig. 1}.

d} Press the binding to the inside on the front side of the sleeve only, and baste the binding in place ½ in/12 mm from the sleeve opening edge. At the top folded edge of the binding, on the wrong side of the sleeve, sew a small diagonal line to help keep the binding folded to the inside {fig. 2}.

e} Machine baste three rows of stitching along the bottom of the sleeve opening and between the front and back notches along the sleeve cap (see instructions for gathering on page 17).

f} Align the sleeve along the underarm edges, wrong-sides together, and pin. Sew the underarm seam together using a French seam (see page 30). Press the seam toward the back of the sleeve.

g} Gather the sleeve opening to approximately the width of the cuff by gently pulling the bobbin threads of the basting stitches. Pin the right side of the sleeve to the right side of the interfaced side of the cuff, aligning the raw edges; make sure not to catch the inside cuff folded edge. Sew together and press the seam allowance toward the cuff. Then slipstitch the inside cuff to the inside of the sleeve cuff seam allowance. Remove any visible basting stitches {fig. 3}.

h} Using the sewing machine buttonhole foot and following the manufacturer's instructions, stitch the buttonhole on the cuff, according to the buttonhole placement marks on the pattern piece. Cut the buttonhole open, and mark through it where the button should be on the opposite end of the cuff. Hand stitch the button in place.

i} Repeat steps 6a through 6h for the second sleeve and cuff.

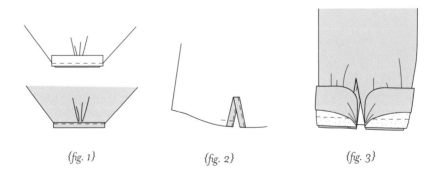

{fig. 1}   {fig. 2}   {fig. 3}

7. Set the sleeves into the armholes.

a} Align a sleeve and an armhole of the dress, right-sides together, making sure to match up all notches and seams, then pin at each notch and seam. Gently pull on the sleeve cap basting threads to ease the sleeve cap into the armhole, adjust the ease evenly, and pin where needed.

b} Machine baste the sleeve to the armhole ½ in/ 12 mm from the edge, making sure there are no visible puckers on the sleeve or armhole stitching line. Once you are happy with how the sleeve is set in place, set the machine to the normal stitch length and sew the sleeve in place ⅝ in/16 mm from the edge {fig. 4}.

c} Remove any visible basting stitches and clip the seam allowances around the armhole. Press the seam allowance toward the dress, and finish the raw edges in your preferred method.

d} Repeat steps 7a through 7c for the second sleeve.

8. Finish the dress.

a} Hand tack the facing to the dress at the shoulder seams with a few small backstitches. Stitch through only the shoulder seam allowances of the dress, so the stitches don't show through to outside of the garment.

b} Fold the center back facing edges under at the crease made in step 3c, and slipstitch the facing edges to the zipper tape.

c} Finger-press the hem under to the wrong side 1½ in/4 cm, and pin in place. Try on the dress to confirm that you like the length and that the hem is even. Make any hem adjustments that may be necessary, then press the hem in place with an iron.

d} Hem the dress following the instructions for a blind hem with seam binding or lace on page 21.

{fig. 4}

MARY VARIATION

The Mary variation dress keeps the same 1960s vibe of the original, but the collar and sleeves have been removed and a bottom band has been added, giving you the perfect opportunity to play with some color blocking.

{front}   {back}

SUGGESTED FABRICS

Wool crepe, gabardine, suiting, or tweed for dress. Rayon Bemberg or china silk for lining.

ADDITIONAL TECHNIQUES

Sewing an all-in-one facing (page 16)

MATERIALS

1½ yd/1.4 m of main fabric (45 in/114 cm wide) *or* ⅞ yd/80 cm of main fabric (60 in/152 cm wide) for dress
¾ yd/70 cm of contrast fabric (45 in/114 cm wide) *or* ⅝ yd/57 cm of contrast fabric (60 in/152 cm wide) for yoke and bands
½ yd/46 cm of lining fabric (45 in/114 cm wide) for facings
1¾ yd/1.6 m of seam binding or lace trim (optional)
One 22-in/56-cm zipper and 1½ yd/1.4 m of fusible web tape (¼ in/6 mm wide)
Coordinating thread

TOOLS

Basic tools (page 10)

1. Trace the following pieces of the Mary pattern: Front, Back, Front Yoke, and Back Yoke. Cut out the traced pattern pieces.

2. Make changes to the front and back pattern pieces as shown in the illustration and described as follows:

a} Cut both pattern pieces along the variation line. Tape extra paper to the bottom of the Front and Back pattern pieces, and add ⅝ in/16 mm for seam allowance.

b} Label the bottom band pieces as "Front Band, Cut 1 contrast fabric on the fold" and "Back Band, Cut 2 contrast fabric." Tape extra paper to the top edge of both Band pieces, and add ⅝ in/16 mm for seam allowance.

3. Lay the pattern pieces on the main and contrast fabrics as shown in the variation layout, and cut them out. Transfer all pattern markings to the fabric pieces after cutting. The front and back yoke are also cut out of lining fabric, and the lining fabric pieces will now be referred to as "front facing" and "back facing."

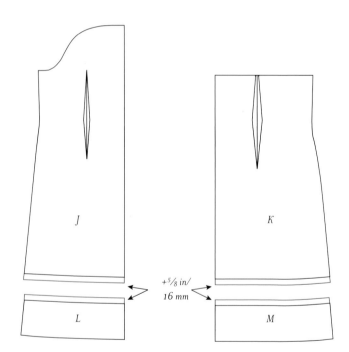

PATTERN PIECE LIST

Front Yoke (C)   Altered Front (J)   Front Band (L)

Back Yoke (D)   Altered Back (K)   Back Band (M)

Note: *The variation pictured on page 118 has the contrast fabric underlined, since the fabric used was loosely woven tweed that I cut on the bias. This step isn't mentioned in the following instructions, since it really depends on what fabric is used for the contrast pieces and how you want to use it. If you use a solid fabric for the contrast then there is no need to cut the pieces on the bias or underline them.*

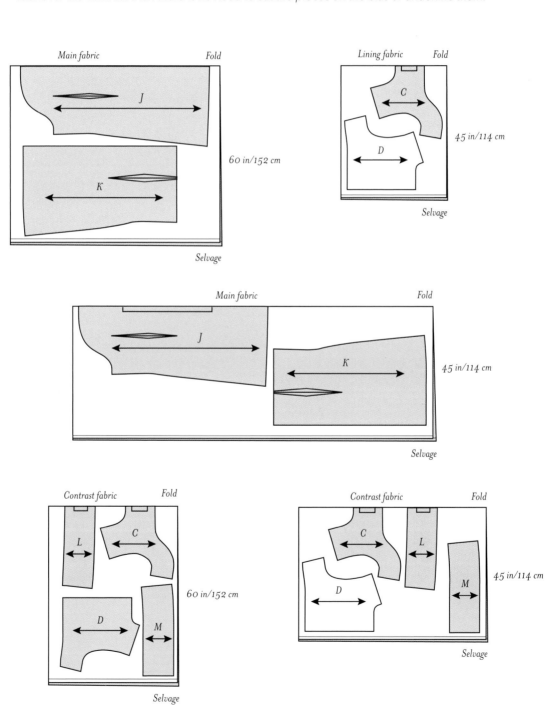

1. Prep the cut-out pieces.

a} Follow step 1a of the Mary dress instructions, but also staystitch around the armholes of the facings. Ignore any reference to the collar and cuff pieces.

2. Sew the darts closed, and attach the yoke and bottom band pieces.

a} Follow steps 2a through 2c of the Mary instructions. Then take the following steps to join the band pieces.

b} Align the top raw edge of one back band to the bottom raw edge of one back body piece, right-sides together, and pin. Sew together, press the seam allowance toward the band, and finish the raw edges in your preferred method. Repeat this step with the second set of back band and back pieces.

c} Repeat step 2b with the front band and front body pieces.

3. Sew the shoulder seams and the all-in-one facing.

a} Follow steps 3a and 3b in the Mary dress instructions, substituting the front and back yokes when referring to the facings. There is also no need to finish either shoulder seam on the dress or facing pieces.

b} Fold and press the center back edges of the back facing under to the wrong side $7/8$ in/2 cm to create a crease, then unfold. Fold and press the bottom raw edges of the facings $5/8$ in/16 mm under to the wrong side to crease, then unfold. Clip the seam allowance at the curves on the front facing bottom edge, where necessary.

c} Align the joined facing piece to the joined front and back dress piece along the neck and armhole edges, right-sides together, and pin. Follow the instructions for sewing an all-in-one facing on page 16 for the facing at the neck and armhole edges. Leave the facing and dress side seams unsewn at this point.

4. Sew the back pieces together, insert a centered zipper, and sew the side seams.

a} Follow step 5a of the Mary dress.

b} Flip the facings up at the side seam, align the facings and the front and back pieces along the side seam edges, right-sides together, and pin. Make sure the armhole, yoke, and band seams are aligned. Sew the side seams together in one continuous seam from the facing edge to the bottom edge of the dress, then press the seam open (see step 4 of sewing an all-in-one facing, page 16). Finish the raw edges in your preferred method. Fold the facing to the inside of the dress and press the neck and armholes flat along the seams.

5. Finish the dress.

a} Fold the center back edges of the back facing under at the crease made in step 3b, and slip-stitch the folded edges to the zipper tape. Then fold the bottom edge of the facing under along the crease made in step 3b, and slipstitch the facing to the yoke seam allowance.

b} With the right side of the dress facing up, top-stitch along the band seam ¼ in/6 mm from the seam on the band side, catching all layers of the seam allowance in the topstitching. Then topstitch around each armhole and the neck opening ¼ in/6 mm from the edge.

c} Finger-press the hem under to the wrong side, 1½ in/4 cm, and pin in place. Try on the dress to confirm that you like the length and that the hem is even. Make any hem adjustments that may be necessary, then press the hem in place with an iron.

d} Hem the dress following the instructions for a blind hem with seam binding or lace on page 21 to finish.

LIZA MINNELLI

"Reality is something you rise above."–**LIZA MINNELLI**

Liza Minnelli epitomizes the sleek side of the ever-diverse 1970s style. This era started with the flower-power hippie look, then moved into flashy disco, and ultimately ended with dramatic punk fashion. Somehow, Liza rose above most of these trends to create a look all her own. She was close friends with designer Halston and called him her "fashion guru." He helped refine her already distinctive style, and she still wears his designs to this day. Liza loves to wear black and bold colors, and has been called the "queen of sequins." You won't see her in a pale, muted shade! This photo of her with her father at the 1970 Oscars sums up her style of that era: short dark hair, bold eye make-up, a chic simple dress, and statement jewelry. The knit wrap dress was debuting as a fashion all-star around this time and quickly became a style staple that is still worn today.

SUGGESTED FABRICS

Polyester blend ITY (interlock twist yarn) jersey, cotton or cotton blend medium-weight jersey, or rayon or polyester blend matte jersey

TECHNIQUES

Sewing knit fabric seams (page 23)
Binding as a facing with knit fabric (page 25)
Hemming knit fabric (page 26)

MATERIALS

2⅛ yd/2 m of main fabric (60 in/152 cm wide) for dress
⅓ yd/30 cm of clear elastic (⅜ in/1 cm wide)
3½ yd/3.2 m of fusible web tape (¼ in/6 mm wide)
Coordinating thread

TOOLS

Basic tools (page 10)
Ball-point or jersey sewing machine needle, size 70/10

{front}   {back}

1. Trace the four Liza pattern pieces from the pattern sheet in the front of the book, in your size. Draft one rectangle onto pattern paper in the following dimensions for the Waist Tie pattern piece, in your size (see Waist Tie Chart for sizing). Label this piece "Waist Tie, Cut 2 main fabric," and place the grainline along the length of the piece.

2. Cut out the traced and drafted pattern pieces.

3. Lay the pattern pieces on the fabric as shown in the fabric layout, and cut them out. Transfer all pattern markings to the fabric pieces after cutting.

4. Cut one 51-in/1.3-m strip of fabric on the lengthwise grain that is 2 in/5 cm wide for the neck facing (see fabric layout). Cut two 23-in/58-cm strips of fabric on the lengthwise grain that are each 2 in/5 cm wide for arm-hole facings.

5. Cut two pieces of clear elastic the same length as the shoulder seam on the pattern.

WAIST TIE CHART

	XS	S	M	L	XL
Length	36 in	39 in	42 in	45 in	48 in
	91 cm	99 cm	107 cm	114 cm	122 cm
Width	4½ in	4½ in	4½ in	4½ in	4½ in
	11 cm	11cm	11 cm	11 cm	11 cm

PATTERN PIECE LIST

Front Bodice (A)   Front Skirt (C)   Waist Tie (E)

Back Bodice (B)   Back Skirt (D)

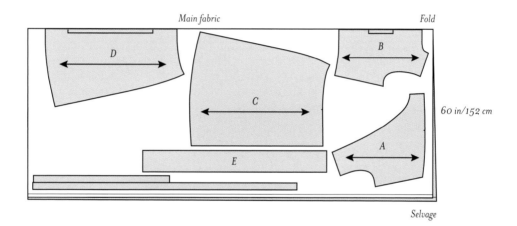

1. Sew the bodice and the skirt together.

a} Align the back bodice and front bodice along the shoulder raw edges, right-sides together, with the front bodice on top. Lay the clear elastic along one shoulder of the front bodice ⅜ in/1 cm from the raw edge, and pin all layers together. Sew the shoulder seam together with a double-stitched seam (see Sewing Knit Fabric Seams, page 23), catching the clear elastic in the stitching. Trim the seam allowance to ⅜ in/ 1 cm. With the right side up, lightly press the shoulder seam toward the back bodice. Repeat this step on the second shoulder.

b} Finish the neck raw edges, following the instructions for binding as a facing with knit fabric on page 25. Do not finish the armhole edges yet.

c} Align the back bodice and back skirt along the waist seam raw edges, right-sides together, and pin. Sew together with a double-stitched seam. Trim the seam allowance to ⅜ in/1 cm and press toward the skirt. Repeat this step on both sides of the front bodice with the front skirt pieces.

2. Sew the armhole facings and side seams.

a} Finish the armhole raw edges, following the instructions for binding as a facing with knit fabric on page 25, stopping after completing step 4.

b} Sew the wearer's left side seam. With the facing flipped up at the armhole and the back piece on top, align the front and back pieces along the raw edges at the right-hand side of the piece, right-sides together. Pin together, making sure to match at the facing edges, the armhole, and waist seams. Starting at the facing edge and ending at bottom edge, sew the side seam together, trim the seam allowance to ⅜ in/1 cm, and press the seam toward the back.

c} Sew the wearer's right side seam. Align as in step 2b, but have the front piece on top. When sewing this side seam together, leave the side seam unsewn between the two notches on the bodice side seam, to create an opening for the waist tie. Make sure to backstitch at the top and bottom of the side seam opening. Press the

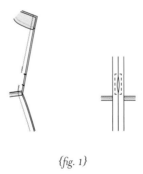

{fig. 1}

seam allowance open at the side seam opening. Sew the seam allowance down at each side of the opening by topstitching a rectangle around the opening ¼ in/6 mm from the folded edges. Trim the rest of the side seam allowance to ⅜ in/ 1 cm, and press the seam allowances above and below the opening toward the back {fig. 1}.

d} Finish sewing the armhole facings by following steps 6 and 7 of the instructions for binding as a facing with knit fabric on page 25.

3. Sew the waist ties, attach to the bodice, and finish the dress.

a} Fold the waist tie in half lengthwise, right-sides together, aligning all raw edges, and pin. Starting at one short end, sew the tie together, pivot, and continue sewing the long raw edges together, and stop sewing at the end of the long seam. Leave the other short end open, trim the seam allowance to ¼ in/6 mm, and turn the tie right-side out through the opening at the short end. Press the tie flat along the fold and seam. Repeat this step for the second waist tie piece.

b} Take one waist tie and align the short open end with the wrong side of the raw front edge of the wearer's left bodice. Pin in place and sew to the bodice ⅜ in/1 cm from the edge. Repeat this step with the second waist tie on the wearer's right bodice raw edge {fig. 2}.

c} Fold and press the bottom raw edge of the skirt ¾ in/2 cm to the wrong side. Follow the instructions for hemming knit fabric on page 26.

d} Fold and press each front raw edge on the skirt and bodice ¾ in/2 cm to the wrong side. Follow the instructions for hemming knit fabric on page 26.

e} Fold each waist tie over the front opening hem, so the ties extend past the front openings. Pin the ties in place and edgestitch each tie to the front opening edges. Slip the dress on, lace the left tie through the opening on the right side seam, then wrap both ties around your body from back to front and tie the ends together at the front.

{fig. 2}

LIZA VARIATION

The Liza variation dress has the addition of sleeves from the Chanel dress and a more swingy skirt. These changes give it the classic 1970s knit wrap dress silhouette, first made famous by Diane von Fürstenberg. The jersey wrap dress's staying power through the decades has a lot to do with how well it flatters many different body types.

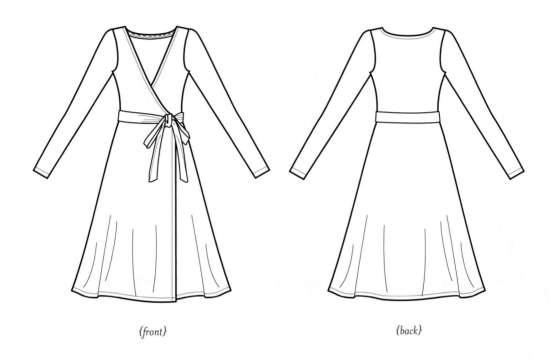

{front}   {back}

SUGGESTED FABRICS

Polyester blend ITY (interlock twist yarn) jersey, cotton or cotton blend medium-weight jersey, or rayon or polyester blend matte jersey

MATERIALS

3¼ yd/3 m of main fabric (60 in/152 cm wide) for dress
⅓ yd/30 cm of clear elastic (⅜ in/1 cm wide)
5 yd/4.6 m of fusible web tape (¼ in/6 mm wide)
Coordinating thread

TOOLS

Basic tools (page 10)
Ball-point or jersey sewing machine needle in size 70/10

1. Trace the four Liza pattern pieces from the pattern sheet in the front of the book, in your size. Then from the Chanel pattern, trace the Sleeve pattern piece, in your size. Follow the Liza dress instructions on how to draft the Waist Tie pattern piece.

2. Cut out the traced pattern pieces. Make changes to the Bodice and Skirt pattern pieces as shown in the illustration and described as follows.

a} Add a ⁵⁄₈ in/16 mm seam allowance evenly to the front and back bodice arm holes.

b} Slash the Front Skirt pattern piece into four approximately equal pieces. Cut the pattern from the hem to the waist seam; don't cut all the way through the waist. Place the slashed pattern onto a new piece of paper and tape the front edge of the pattern in place. Spread the pattern pieces apart at the first slash so that the bottom edges are 2 in/5 cm apart, and tape them in place. Repeat at each slash, adding a total of 6 in/15 cm to the bottom edge. The waist seam should remain the same measurement.

c} Repeat the preceding step with the Back Skirt pattern piece, except you will only slash it into three pieces. There will be a total of 4 in/10 cm added to the Back Skirt bottom edge.

3. Lay the pattern pieces on the fabric as shown in the fabric layout, and cut them out. Transfer all pattern markings to the fabric pieces after cutting.

4. Cut one 51-in/1.3-m strip of fabric on the length-wise grain that is 2 in/5 cm wide for the neck facing.

5. Cut two pieces of clear elastic the same length as the shoulder seam on the pattern.

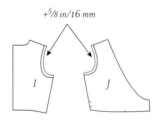

+⁵⁄₈ in/16 mm

+2 in/5 cm

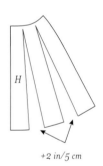

+2 in/5 cm

PATTERN PIECE LIST

Waist Tie (E)

Sleeve (H)
(from Chanel pattern)

Altered Front Bodice (I)

Altered Back Bodice (J)

Altered Front Skirt (L)

Altered Back Skirt (M)

1. Sew the bodice, sleeves, and skirt together.

a} Follow steps 1a and 1b of the Liza dress instructions.

b} Align one sleeve and one bodice armhole along the raw edges, right-sides together, and pin them along the seam line, being careful not to stretch either piece out of shape. Sew the sleeve to the bodice, press the seam allowance toward the sleeve, and trim to ⅜ in/1 cm. Repeat on the opposite armhole with the other sleeve.

c} Follow step 1c of the Liza dress instructions.

2. Sew the side seams and the underarms.

a} Fold the bottom sleeve edge up ¾ in/2 cm toward the wrong side of the fabric, and press a crease, then unfold.

b} Sew the wearer's left side seam. With the back piece on top, align the front and back pieces along the raw edges at the right-hand side of the pieces, right-sides together, then align the sleeve underarm raw edges. Pin together, making sure to match the pieces at the armhole and waist seams. Starting at the bottom skirt edge and ending at the bottom sleeve edge, sew the side seam together, trim the seam allowance to ⅜ in/1 cm, and press toward the back.

c} Follow step 2c of the Liza dress instructions but align the sleeve underarm raw edges and sew together starting from the bottom skirt and ending at the bottom sleeve edge.

3. Sew the waist ties, attach to the bodice, and finish the dress.

a} Follow steps 3a through 3e of the Liza dress instructions. At step 3c, also hem the sleeve bottom edges for this variation.

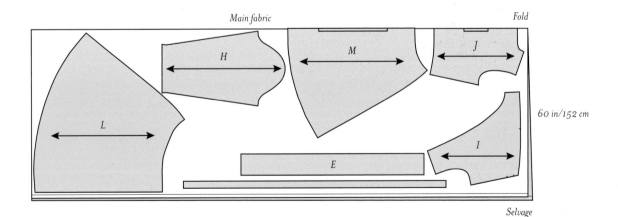

Main fabric

Fold

60 in/152 cm

Selvage

ANJELICA HUSTON

"There were times when I hated my nose. But you grow up and you start to recognize that maybe it wasn't a bad thing that you weren't born Barbie."–**ANJELICA HUSTON**

Anjelica Huston represents refined sophistication. She has a strong sense of style and her look hasn't changed much over the years. She favors chic jewel-toned dresses, monochromatic pantsuits, and, of course, those red lips! Even during the excess of the 1980s (when this picture was taken) she managed to pull off a simple, timeless look. This dress gives a nod to the 1980s with its play on proportion–it is a bit oversized on top and more slim-fitting around the hips. It is made in a matte jersey fabric that's simple to sew and easy to care for. You'll just need a hip-slung belt and cute shoes to finish it off.

SUGGESTED FABRICS

Rayon or polyester blend matte jersey, medium-weight cotton or cotton blend jersey, or polyester blend
ITY (interlock twist yarn) jersey

TECHNIQUES

Sewing knit fabric seams (page 23)
Binding as a facing with knit fabric (page 25)
Hemming knit fabric (page 26)

MATERIALS

1½ yd/1.4 m of main fabric (60 in/152 cm wide) for dress
½ yd/46 cm of clear elastic (³⁄₈ in/1 cm wide)
2 yd/1.8 m of fusible web tape (¼ in/6 mm wide)
Coordinating thread

TOOLS

Basic tools (page 10)
Ball-point or jersey sewing machine needle in size 70/10

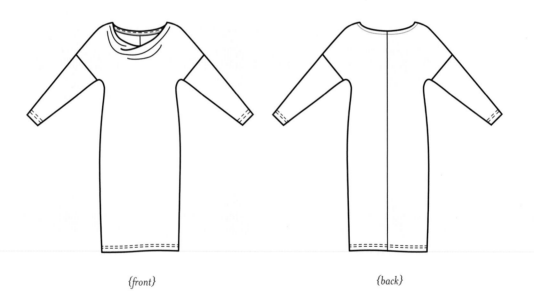

{front}   {back}

1. Trace the three Anjelica pattern pieces from the pattern sheet in the front of the book, in your size, but omit the darts on the pattern (the darts are for the variation). Cut out the traced pattern pieces.

2. Lay the pattern pieces on the fabric as shown in the fabric layout, and cut them out. Transfer all pattern markings to the fabric pieces after cutting.

3. Cut one 14-in/35.5-cm strip of fabric on the lengthwise grain that is 2 in/5 cm wide for the back neck facing.

4. Cut two pieces of clear elastic about 5 in/12 cm long.

PATTERN PIECE LIST

Front (A)   Back (B)   Sleeve (C)

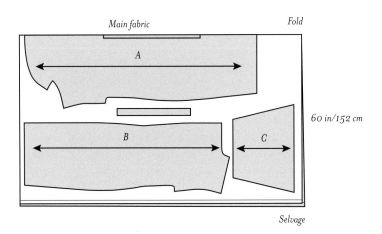

1. Sew the back and finish the back neck.

a} Align both back pieces along the center back seam, right-sides together, and pin. Sew together, with a double-stitched seam (see Sewing Knit Fabric Seams, page 23). Trim the seam allowance to ⅜ in/1 cm and press to one side.

b} Using a zigzag stitch, baste the clear elastic onto the wrong side of the back shoulders ⅜ in/1 cm from the raw edge.

c} Finish the back neck edge, following the instructions for binding as a facing with knit fabric, page 25.

2. Sew the body and the sleeves.

a} Using a zigzag stitch, finish the top raw edge on the front piece. This edge will fold inside the garment to form the cowl neck.

b} Lay the back piece on top of the front, right-sides together, and align all raw edges except at the front cowl neck {fig. 1}. Fold the cowl back at the shoulder and align the shoulder raw edges on top of the back piece. Part of the back shoulders should be sandwiched between the front and the cowl fold back.

Pin the shoulders together and sew through all layers with a double-stitched seam (see page 23). Trim the seam allowance to ⅜ in/1 cm, and press it toward the front {fig. 2}.

c} Align one sleeve top raw edge along one armhole raw edge, right-sides together, and pin. The sleeve is about ½ in/12 mm smaller than the armhole, so to get the sleeve to fit the armhole, just stretch the sleeve a bit. Sew the sleeve to the armhole, trim the seam allowance to ⅜ in/1 cm, and press toward the sleeve. Repeat this step for the second sleeve.

d} Align the side seam and the underarm seam raw edges, right-sides together, and pin, making sure to match up the seams at the armhole. Sew the side seam together, starting at the bottom and ending at the bottom of the sleeve. Trim the seam allowance to ⅜ in/1 cm, and press toward the back. Repeat the step for the second side seam.

3. Finish the dress.

a} Fold and press the sleeve and dress bottom edges over ¾ in/2 cm to the wrong side, and sew the hems following the instructions for hemming knit fabric on page 26.

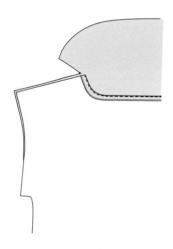

{fig. 1}

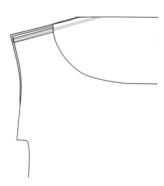

{fig. 2}

ANJELICA VARIATION

The Anjelica variation is another great separate. While the Anjelica dress is made from a knit fabric, this blouse is made from a lightweight woven fabric that is cut on the bias for a little extra give. To achieve a slightly boxy fit that would look great with jeans, omit the darts.

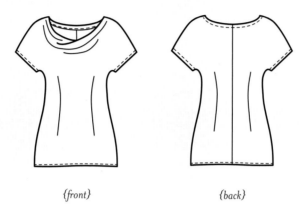

{front}   *{back}*

SUGGESTED FABRICS

Silk, rayon or polyester blend crepe de chine or charmeuse, cotton lawn, or voile

ADDITIONAL TECHNIQUES

Darts (page 15)
French seam (page 30)
Baby hem (page 20)

MATERIALS

2 yd/1.8 m of main fabric (45 in/114 cm wide) for blouse
Coordinating thread

SUPPLIES

Basic tools (page 10)

1. Trace the Front and Back Anjelica pattern pieces from the pattern sheet in the front of the book, in your size. Trace only to the short variation length on the pattern, and trace the dart markings if you are using darts. Cut out the traced pattern pieces.

2. Lay the pattern pieces on the fabric as shown in the fabric layout, and cut them out. Transfer all pattern markings to the fabric pieces after cutting.

3. Cut one 15-in-/38-cm-long strip of fabric on the bias grain that is 1 in/2.5 cm wide, for the back neck facing. Press the strip into single-fold binding (see page 12).

PATTERN PIECE LIST

Front (A)   Back (B)

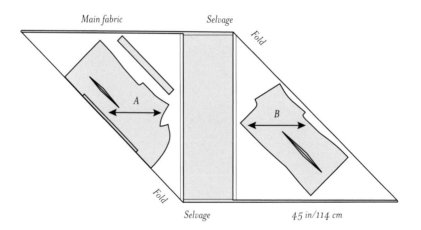

144

1. Sew the darts and the back.

a} Sew all the darts closed (see page 15) on the front and back pieces.

b} Align the back pieces along the center back edges, wrong-sides together, and pin. Sew the center back seam together using the French seam technique (see page 30) and press to one side.

c} Finish the back neck with modified binding as facing, using the instructions as follows. Unfold one long edge of the single-fold bias tape, align the raw edges at the back neck, and pin in place. With the wrong side of the bias tape facing up, stitch along the first crease line, which should be about ¼ in/6 mm from the edge. Clip the seam allowance around the neck curve, being careful not to cut into the stitching. Fold and press the bias tape toward the neck opening, wrap the bias tape to the wrong side of the back, and press along the seam. Then edgestitch through all layers, along the inner fold of the bias tape, making sure there are no puckers in the garment fabric.

2. Sew the body together and finish the edges.

a} Finish the top raw edge on the front piece in your preferred method. This edge will fold inside the garment to form the cowl neck.

b} Lay the back piece on top of the front, aligning all raw edges except at the front cowl neck *{fig. 1}*. Fold the cowl back at the shoulder and align the shoulder raw edges on top of the back piece. Part of the back shoulders should be sandwiched between the front and the cowl fold back. Pin the shoulders together, and sew through all layers. Press the seam allowance toward the front, and finish the raw edges in your preferred method *{fig. 2}*.

c} Align the raw edges of one of the side seams, right-sides together, and pin. Sew the side seam together, starting from the bottom and ending at the armhole. Clip the seam allowance at the armhole curve, and press the seam open. Finish the raw edges in your preferred method. Repeat this step on second side seam.

d} Hem the armhole openings with a baby hem (see page 20).

e} Hang the garment for 24 hours before hemming the bottom edge. After hanging the garment, check to see if the bottom edge is even, and trim to make it even, if necessary. Hem the bottom opening with a baby hem (see page 20).

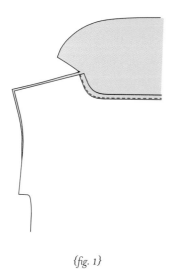

{fig. 1}

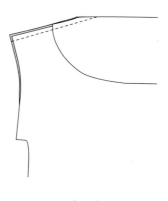

{fig. 2}

PRINCESS DIANA

"I don't go by the rule book. . . . I lead from the heart, not the head."–**PRINCESS DIANA**

Princess Diana was admired for her understated feminine glamour. She went from a shy, blushing teacher's assistant to a fashion icon the moment her engagement to Prince Charles was announced. I will never forget watching the royal wedding in 1981 and seeing her quintessential princess wedding dress with the very long train. I was a little girl at the time and fell completely in love with that dress! Her style evolved and became more elegant and classic over time. By the 1990s, she preferred simple, chic clothes that flattered her figure. This boatneck dress can be dressed up or down depending on your mood. Pair it with flats and a soft cardigan for brunch with friends, or with kitten heels and a scarf for date night.

SUGGESTED FABRICS

Cotton piqué, medium-weight cotton poplin, linen, lightweight wool, or denim for dress.
Rayon Bemberg or china silk for lining.

TECHNIQUES

Princess seams (page 29)
How to line a dress (page 27)
Centered zipper (page 34)
Blind hemming with seam binding or lace (page 21)
Baby hem (page 20)

MATERIALS

2¼ yd/2.1 m of main fabric (45 in/114 cm wide) *or* 1⅞ yd/1.7 m of main fabric (60 in/152 cm wide) for dress
2¼ yd/2.1 m of fabric (45 in/114 cm) for lining
1¾ yd/1.6 m of seam binding or lace trim (optional)
One 22-in/56-cm zipper and 1½ yd/1.4 m of fusible web tape (¼ in/6 mm wide)
Coordinating thread

TOOLS

Basic tools (page 10)

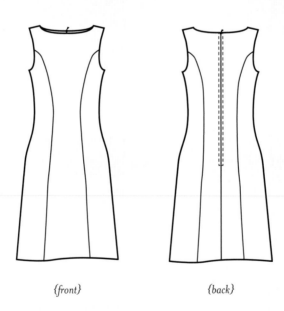

{front}   {back}

1. Trace the four Diana pattern pieces from the pattern sheet in the front of the book, in your size. Cut out the traced pattern pieces.

2. Lay the pattern pieces on the fabric as shown in the fabric layout. Cut the four pieces out of both the dress fabric and the lining fabric. Transfer all pattern markings to the fabric pieces after cutting.

PATTERN PIECE LIST

Front (A)

Back (B)

Side Front (C)

Side Back (D)

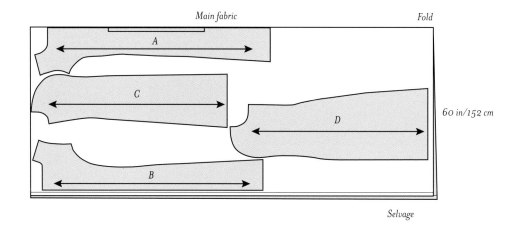

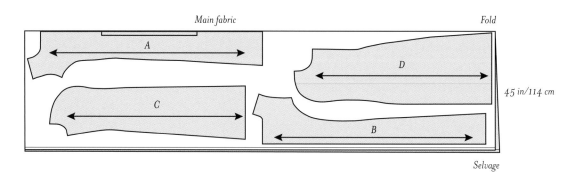

1. Prep the cut-out pieces.

a} Staystitch the neckline and armholes on the front and back pieces ½ in/12 mm from the edge. Staystitch the armholes on the side front and side back pieces ½ in/12 mm from the edge. Repeat this step on the lining pieces.

2. Sew the princess seams and shoulder seams, and attach the lining.

a} Align the front and side front pieces along the princess seams, right-sides together, and follow the instructions for sewing a princess seam on page 29. There's no need to finish the raw edges. Repeat this step for the front lining pieces.

b} Repeat step 2a with the back and back lining pieces; the back pieces don't have any ease added to the princess seam.

c} Align the front and back pieces along the shoulder raw edges, right-sides together, and pin. Sew the shoulders together, and press open. There's no need to finish the raw edges.

d} Repeat step 2c on the front and back lining pieces.

e} Prepare the center back seam allowance on the back lining pieces. Fold over and press the center back seam allowance to the wrong side ⅞ in/2 cm. Unfold the lining center back seam edges, leaving a pressed crease.

f} Align the joined lining piece to the joined dress piece along the neck and armhole edges, right-sides together. Pin along the neck and armhole edges, then follow the sewing instructions for how to line a dress on page 27. Leave the lining and dress side seams unsewn at this point.

3. Insert a centered zipper and sew the side seams.

a} Flip the lining up and out of the way, so it isn't caught in the center back seam or zipper stitching, and don't sew or baste the lining center seam together at this point. Align the center back seam along the raw edges, right-sides

together, and pin. Follow the instructions for a centered zipper on page 34. Make sure that the top of the zipper teeth is about ⅛ in/3 mm below the back neck seam line. There's no need to finish the raw edges.

b} Flip the lining up at one side seam, so the bottom edges of the lining are positioned above the armholes. Align the front and back lining pieces and then the front and back dress pieces along the side seam raw edges, right-sides together, and pin. Making sure that the armhole seams are matched up, sew the lining and dress side seams together in one continuous seam and press it open (just like step 4 of sewing an all-in-one facing, page 16). Repeat on opposite side seam.

c} Align the lining center back seam along the raw edges, right-sides together, and pin from the bottom edge to the zipper notches. Sew the bottom lining back seam together; stop and backstitch at the notches. Press the seam open. There's no need to finish the raw edges. Turn the lining to the inside of the dress and press the seams flat at the armholes.

4. Finish the dress.

a} Fold the back lining edges under at the crease made in step 2e, and slipstitch the lining folded edges to the zipper tape.

b} Finger-press the hem under to the wrong side 1½ in/4 cm, and pin in place. Try on the dress to confirm that you like the length and that the hem is even. Make any hem adjustments that may be necessary, then press the hem in place with an iron.

c} Hem the dress following the instructions for making a blind hem with seam binding or lace on page 21.

d} Trim the bottom edge of the lining so it is about ½ in/12 mm shorter than the finished dress, then hem it to the wrong side with a baby hem (see page 20).

DIANA VARIATION

The Diana variation is a separate top that can be worn with the Joan variation bias-cut skirt (page 67) or the Grace variation pencil skirt (page 105). By shortening the dress, reshaping the neck, adding side vents, and changing the closure at center back to buttons, you end up with an attractive shell that looks great under a blazer for work or with a pair of shorts for a weekend outing.

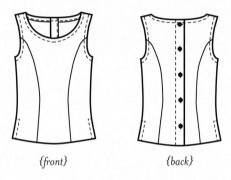

{front}   *{back}*

SUGGESTED FABRICS

Silk or polyester crepe, cotton shirting, lightweight cotton poplin, or linen

ADDITIONAL TECHNIQUES

Binding as a facing with single-fold bias tape (page 13)
Narrow clean-finish hem (page 21)

MATERIALS

1½ yd/1.4 m of main fabric (45 in/114 cm wide) *or* 1⅜ yd/1.3 m of main fabric (60 in/152 cm wide) for shell
¾ yd/70 cm lightweight fusible interfacing (20 in/50 cm wide)
Six ⅝-in/16-mm buttons
Coordinating thread

SUPPLIES

Basic tools (page 10)

1. Trace the four Diana pattern pieces from the pattern sheet in the front of the book, in your size, but only trace to the short variation length on the pattern. Also trace the Diana variation Buttonhole Template from the pattern sheet.

2. Make the changes to the pattern pieces as shown in the following illustration and described as follows:

a} Drop the front neck 2 in/5 cm, then bring the front neck width out ½ in/12 mm and draw a new front neckline. Trim ½ in/12 mm evenly from the front armhole.

b} Trim ½ in/12 mm evenly off the back neck and back armhole. Add 2 in/5 cm to the center back.

c} Add vent notches on the side front and side back pieces 4 in/10 cm up from bottom edge, at the side seams.

3. Cut out the traced and altered pattern pieces.

4. Lay the pattern pieces on the fabric as shown in the fabric layout, and cut them out. Transfer all pattern markings to the fabric pieces after cutting.

5. Cut enough 1-in-/2.5-cm-wide bias strips so that when they are pieced together they equal at least 92 in/234 cm long (see instructions for making your own single-fold bias tape, page 12).

6. Cut out two strips of interfacing, 1½ in/4 cm wide, that equal the length of the center back pattern piece.

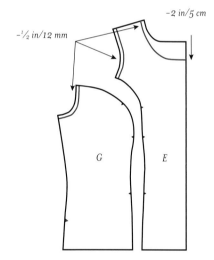

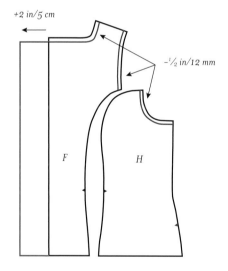

PATTERN PIECE LIST

Altered Front (E)　　　　Altered Side Front (G)　　　　Buttonhole Template

Altered Back (F)　　　　Altered Side Back (H)

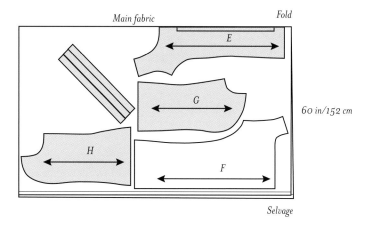

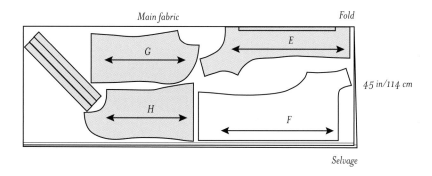

1. Prepare the cut-out pieces.

a} Follow step 1a of the Diana dress instructions, except do the staystitching ⅛ in/3 mm from the raw edge.

b} Baste or fuse the interfacing to the wrong side of each back piece along the center back edge.

c} Press the bias strips into single-fold bias tape (see page 12).

d} Make clips at the vent notches ⅜ to ½ in/10 to 12 mm long, along the side seam.

2. Sew the princess seams, shoulder seams, and the back placket.

a} To sew the princess seams and shoulder seams, follow steps 2a through 2c of the Diana dress instructions, but ignore any reference to the lining pieces. Finish the raw edges of the princess seams and shoulder seams in your preferred method.

b} Fold under and press the back opening raw edges ⅝ in/16 mm to the wrong side. Then fold and press the edges under again 1 in/2.5 cm {fig. 1}. Edgestitch along the inner folded edges of the center back opening to stitch the placket in place {fig. 2}.

3. Sew the binding, side seams, and side vents.

a} Sew single-fold bias tape to the neckline following the instructions for binding as a facing on page 13. The bias tape will start and stop at each back edge, so the bias tape ends will need to be folded under so they are finished. To do this, measure the entire neckline from the center back edge around to the opposite back edge and add 1 in/2.5 cm to that measurement. Cut the bias tape to the neckline length (plus 1 in/2.5 cm). Fold and press each short end of the bias tape to the wrong side ½ in/ 12 mm, then sew the bias tape in place following the instructions, making sure that each bias tape folded end aligns with the center back edge.

b} Align one of the shell's side seam's raw edges, right-sides together, and pin. Starting from the top of the side seam, sew the side seam together, stopping ¼ in/6 mm below the vent notch. Press the seam open and finish the raw edges above the vent notch in your preferred method. Repeat this step for the opposite side seam.

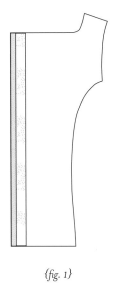

{fig. 1}

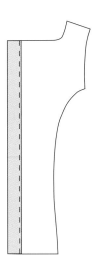

{fig. 2}

c} Sew single-fold bias tape to the armholes, following the instructions for binding as facing on page 13. When you reach the folded end of the bias tape as directed in step 2, continue sewing the bias tape overlapping the folded end by ¾ in/2 cm. Cut off excess bias tape and continue on to step 3. When the bias tape is turned to the inside of the garment, the overlapped section should be covered by the folded end, so no raw edges are exposed.

d} Hem the side vents. Fold under and press each side vent raw edge ¼ in/6 mm to the wrong side, then fold and press the edge under again ⅜ in/1 cm. Fold under and press the top raw edges of each vent at a slight angle and pin the vent hems in place. Starting at one bottom edge of the vent, edgestitch along the inner folded edge, pivoting around the top of vent, and continue stitching down the other side of the vent {fig. 3}. Repeat to sew the second side vent.

4. Sew the buttonholes, sew on the buttons, and finish the shell.

a} Using the buttonhole template, transfer the buttonhole placement to the wearer's left side of the back placket. Following your sewing machine's instructions for using the buttonhole foot, stitch the buttonholes along the markings on the left back placket. Cut the buttonholes open, being careful not to cut the stitches at the ends. Lay the left back placket on top of the right back placket, overlapping just slightly more than 1 in/2.5 cm, so the placket stitching on the right back placket is hidden. Mark where the buttons should go, using the buttonholes as a template.

b} Hand sew the buttons in place.

c} Hem the shell following the instructions for a narrow clean-finish hem on page 21.

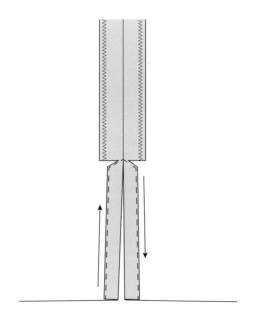

{fig. 3}

KATE MOSS

"I would have wanted to be a rock star, a lead singer, if I wasn't a model. I'd go touring in a bus with my band. In my next life, that's the plan." –**KATE MOSS**

Kate Moss burst onto the modeling scene as a seventeen-year-old girl and launched the waif look of the early 1990s. Since then, she's become a true style icon. From her rock 'n' roll bohemian looks, like ripped jeans shorts and wild fur coats, to the ultra-glamorous red-carpet gowns, Kate keeps us on our toes. For all her different looks, the one thing she does maintain is her effortless style—the tousled hair, the bare face, the simplicity. This stretch lace dress represents Kate's understated glamour. It has a high neckline and long sleeves, but the short length and perfect fit give it a little edge and make it a showstopper.

SUGGESTED FABRICS

4-way stretch lace for dress and sleeves. Silk or polyester blend charmeuse, crepe, or poplin fabric with small amount of stretch for underlining.

TECHNIQUES

Binding as a facing with single-fold bias tape (page 13)
Darts (page 15)
Centered zipper (page 34)
Sewing knit fabric seams (page 23)
Hemming knit fabric (page 26)
Narrow clean-finish hem (page 21)

MATERIALS

1⅞ yd/1.7 m of main fabric (60 in/152 cm wide) for dress and sleeves
2¼ yd/2.1 m of fabric (45 in/114 cm wide) *or* 1⅛ yd/1 m of fabric (60 in/152 cm wide) for underlining
One 22-in/56-cm zipper and 1½ yd/1.4 m of fusible web tape (¼ in/6 mm wide)
1 small hook-and-eye set
Coordinating thread

TOOLS

Basic tools (page 10)

Note: *Since the stretch lace is a knit fabric, you will need to sew it as a knit where it isn't underlined. Use a narrow zigzag stitch at the underarm seam and the bottom hem as you would for a knit fabric. You do not need to use a ball-point needle for this project.*

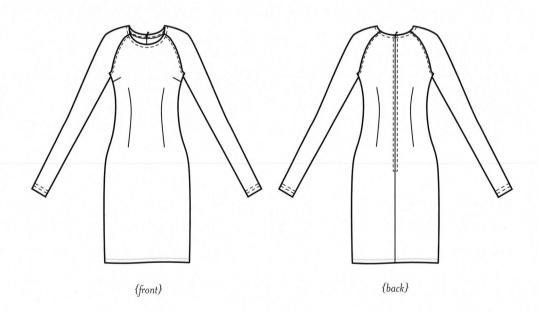

{front}   *{back}*

1. Trace the three Kate pattern pieces from the pattern sheet in the front of the book, in your size. Cut out the traced pattern pieces.

2. Lay the pattern pieces on the main fabric and underlining fabric as shown in the fabric layout, and cut them out. Transfer all pattern markings to the underlining fabric pieces after cutting.

3. Cut one 24-in-/61-cm-long strip of fabric on the bias grain that is 1 in/2.5 cm wide for the neck facing, from the underlining fabric.

PATTERN PIECE LIST

Front (A)   Back (B)   Sleeve (C)

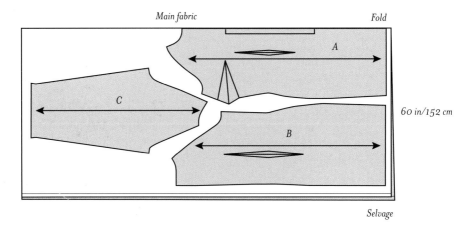

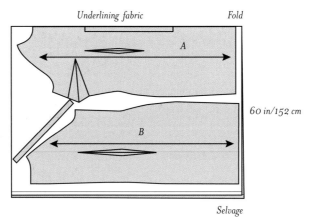

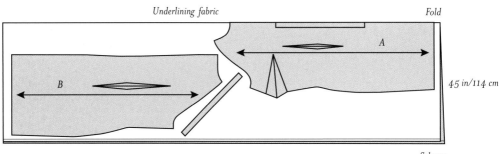

1. Prepare the cut-out pieces.

a} Align all edges of the front and front underlining pieces (see page 27), wrong side of the front to the right side of the front underlining, and pin together. Hand baste the dart markings through both layers of fabric. Then hand or machine baste both layers together at the side seams and armholes ½ in/12 mm from the edge. These two pieces will now be treated as one and called the "front." Repeat with the back and the back underlining pieces; now called the "back."

b} Staystitch the neck edges on the sleeve, front, and back pieces ⅛ in/3 mm from the edge.

c} Press the bias strip into single-fold binding (see page 13).

2. Sew the darts and the center back, and insert a centered zipper.

a} Sew all the darts closed (see page 15) on the back and front pieces.

b} Align the back pieces along the center back raw edges, right-sides together, and pin. Insert a centered zipper following the instructions on page 34, and making sure that the top of the zipper teeth is about ⅞ in/2 cm from the neck raw edge on the back pieces.

3. Sew the sleeves and attach the binding to the neck edge.

a} Align one armhole of the front with the front armhole of one sleeve along the raw edges, right-sides together, and pin. Sew the pieces together along the seam line; clip the seam allowance of the front piece. Press the seam allowance toward the body and finish the raw edges in your preferred method. Repeat for the other sleeve on the opposite front armhole. Then with the right side of the dress facing up, topstitch along the armhole seams ¼ in/6 mm from the seam on the body side. Repeat this step with the back pieces and the back sleeve armholes.

b} Sew the single-fold bias tape to the neckline following the instructions for binding as a facing on page 13. The bias tape will start and stop at each center back edge, so the short bias tape ends will need to be folded under so

they are finished. To do this, measure the entire neckline from the center back edge around to the center back edge, and add 1 in/2.5 cm to that measurement. Cut the bias tape to the neckline length (plus 1 in/2.5 cm). Fold and press each short end to the wrong side ½ in/12 mm, then sew it in place following the instructions, making sure that each bias tape folded end aligns with the center back edge. Make sure not to stretch the lace neck edges of the sleeve when pinning and sewing the bias tape in place.

c} Hand sew the hook-and-eye set to the *inside* of the top center back neck edges. Stitch each in place to the binding only, so the stitching isn't visible from the outside of the garment.

4. Sew the underarms and side seams, and finish the dress.

a} Fold the bottom sleeve edge up ¾ in/2 cm toward the wrong side of the fabric, and press a crease. Leave the sleeve edge unfolded.

b} Align one side seam and underarm seam, raw edges and right-sides together, and pin, making sure to match up the seams at the armhole. Sew the side seam together in one continuous seam, starting at the bottom edge of the sleeve and ending at the bottom edge of the dress. Use a narrow zigzag stitch on the sleeve underarm seam to the armhole, then when you reach the armhole, change to a regular straight stitch. Press the side seam open on the body and finish the raw edges in your preferred method. Trim the sleeve seam allowance down to ⅜ in/1 cm. Repeat this step for the opposite side seam.

c} Fold one sleeve bottom edge under ¾ in/2 cm to the wrong side and hem, following the instructions for hemming a knit fabric on page 26. Repeat this step for the opposite sleeve.

d} Make sure both layers of the dress bottom edges are even; trim if necessary to make both layers even. Then hem both layers as one, following the instructions for a narrow clean-finish hem on page 21, but make each fold ⅛ in/3 mm wider and use a narrow zigzag stitch instead of a straight stitch to finish.

KATE VARIATION

The Kate variation has a totally different feel to it than the original and would be a great summer dress. For this design, I removed the sleeves, added a yoke at the neck, and added a bottom band to the hem. These small details offer a great opportunity to explore color and texture in your fabric choices.

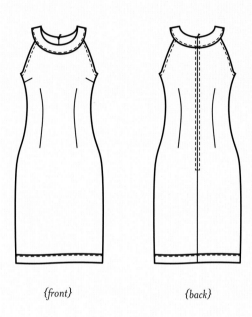

{front}   *{back}*

SUGGESTED FABRICS

Medium-weight linen, linen blend, cotton poplin, cotton piqué, or cotton twill

MATERIALS

2 yd/1.8 m of main fabric (45 in/114 cm) *or* 1 yd/1 m of main fabric (60 in/152 cm wide) for dress
1 yd/1 m of contrast fabric (45 in/114 cm or 60 in/152 cm wide) for yoke and bottom band
½ yd/46 cm of lightweight interfacing (20 in/50 cm wide)
One 22-in/56-cm zipper and 1½ yd/1.4 m of fusible web tape (¼ in/6 mm wide)
Coordinating thread

TOOLS

Basic tools (page 10)

1. Trace the Kate variation pattern pieces, in your size: Front Yoke and Back Yoke. Then trace the following pieces of the Kate pattern, in your size: Front and Back.

2. Make changes to the pattern as shown in the illustration and described in the following steps.

a} Cut the front and back pieces along the variation lines at the top and bottom of the pieces. Discard the top cut-off pieces.

b} Tape extra paper to the top and bottom cut edges of the front and back pieces, and then add a ⅝-in/16-mm seam allowance at each of these edges.

c} Trim ½ in/12 mm evenly off the front and back armholes.

d} Tape extra paper to the top cut edge of each of the cut-off bottom body pieces, and then add a ⅝-in/16-mm seam allowance to each of these edges. Label the piece cut off from the front "Front Band, Cut 2 Contrast fabric on the fold." Label the piece cut off from the back "Back Band, Cut 4 Contrast fabric."

3. Cut out the traced and altered pattern pieces. Lay the pattern pieces on the fabric as shown in the fabric layout, and cut them out. Transfer all pattern markings to the fabric pieces after cutting.

4. Cut two 24-in-/61-cm-long strips from the dress fabric on the bias grain that are 1 in/2.5 cm wide, for armhole facings.

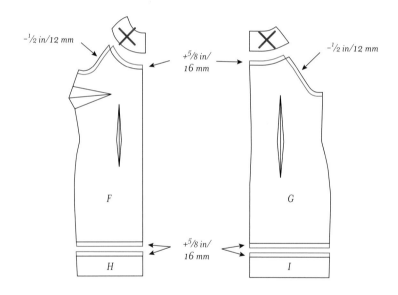

PATTERN PIECE LIST

Front Yoke (D)   Altered Front (F)   Front Band (H)

Back Yoke (E)   Altered Back (G)   Back Band (I)

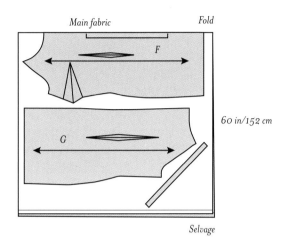

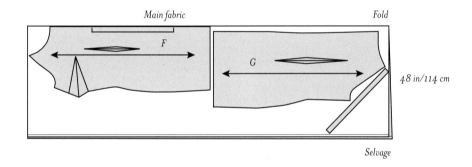

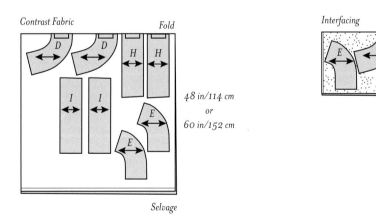

1. Prepare the cut-out pieces.

a} Staystitch the neck edges of the front and back pieces ½ in/12 mm from the raw edges. Staystitch the neck and outer edges of the front and back yoke pieces ½ in/12 mm from the raw edges.

b} Staystitch the armhole edges of the front and back pieces ⅛ in/3 mm from the raw edges.

c} Baste or fuse the interfacing to one set of front and back yoke (mirror image) pieces. The non-interfaced yoke pieces will now be referred to as the "front yoke lining" and "back yoke lining."

d} Follow step 1c of the Kate dress instructions for both armhole facing strips.

2. Sew the darts, side seams, and finish armholes.

a} Follow step 2a of the Kate dress instructions.

b} Align the front and back body pieces along the side seam raw edges, right-sides together, and pin. Sew together, press the seams open, and finish the raw edges in your preferred method.

c} Sew the single-fold binding to the armholes, beginning and ending at the upper raw edges; follow the instructions for binding as a facing on page 13. There is no need to fold back any short end of the single-fold binding, because the binding raw ends will be caught in the yoke seam. Cut off any excess length of binding, so it is even with the body raw edge.

3. Sew the yoke to the body.

a} Fold and press the outer yoke lining raw edge under to the wrong side ⅝ in/16 mm, and clip this seam allowance around the curves. Then fold and press the center back yoke lining edges under to the wrong side ⅞ in/2 cm, to create a crease, but leave unfolded.

b} Align the front and back yoke pieces along the shoulder seam raw edges, right-sides together, and pin. Sew together and press the seams open. Repeat this step for the front and back yoke lining pieces.

c} Align the front to the front yoke along the neck raw edges, placing the front between notches on the front yoke, right-sides together, and pin. Sew together, clip the seam allowances, and press the seam allowance toward the yoke. Repeat this step with the back and back yoke.

d} Clip the seam allowance of the yoke outer raw edges, then press the raw edges under to the wrong side ⅝ in/16 mm between the front and back seams (where the yoke goes over the shoulders) {fig. 1}.

e} Align the yoke and yoke lining along the neck edge, right-sides together, matching the shoulder seams and center back edges, and pin. Sew together, grade the seam allowances, and clip the seam allowance around the curves. Turn the yoke lining to the inside of the dress and press flat along the neck seam.

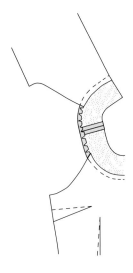

{fig. 1}

4. Sew the center back, insert a centered zipper, and attach the bands.

a} Follow step 2b of the Kate dress instructions, making sure to fold the yoke lining out of the way so it doesn't get caught in the center back seam or zipper stitching. Also make sure the top of the zipper teeth is ⅛ in/3 mm below the top edge of the yoke neck seam.

b} Align the front band with the back band pieces at each side seam, right-sides together, and pin. Sew together and press the seam allowance open. Then align both back band pieces at the center back edge, right-sides together, and pin. Sew together and press the seam allowance open. Repeat for the second set of band pieces.

c} Align one joined band piece with the other along the bottom edges, right-sides together, and pin. Sew together, making sure to match the side and center back seams. Press the seam allowance open, then fold the band pieces, wrong-sides together, and press flat along the bottom seam. Baste the top of the band pieces together ½ in/12 mm from the raw edge.

d} Align the band piece with the bottom of the dress along the raw edges, right-sides together, matching the seams at the side and center back, and pin. Sew together, press the seam allowance toward the band, and finish the raw edges in your preferred method.

e} Topstitch around the band seam ⅛ in/3 mm from the seam on the band side.

5. Finish the dress.

a} Fold the yoke lining center back edges under along the creases made in step 3a. With these edges folded under, align the yoke lining and yoke folded edges at the shoulders, and pin together. Pin the yoke lining along the front and back yoke seam, covering the seam allowance. With the yoke lining facing up, baste all layers together along the outer yoke lining edge, making sure the folded edges at the shoulders match up. Turn the dress right-side out and top-stitch through all layers ⅛ in/3 mm from the yoke outer edge, starting and stopping stitching at the zipper stitching. Remove any visible basting stitches.

b} Slipstitch the yoke lining center back folded edge to the zipper tape to finish.

RESOURCES

BOOKS

Sewing books provide inspiration and are a great way to brush up on skills and techniques. Here are some of my favorites.

GENERAL SEWING BOOKS

THE COLETTE SEWING HANDBOOK
by Sarai Mitnick
A good book for those new to sewing who want to make their own garments. Has helpful information on selecting fabric, fit, and patternmaking.

GERTIE'S NEW BOOK FOR BETTER SEWING
by Gretchen Hirsch
A valuable resource if you are into vintage styles and couture sewing techniques. There are a lot of fun projects in this book.

LINEN AND COTTON: CLASSIC SEWING TECHNIQUES FOR GREAT RESULTS
by Susan Khalje
This book is a perfect alternative if you don't want to invest in Bridal Couture (listed below). It covers a lot of couture techniques and applies them to more casual attire.

COUTURE SEWING BOOKS

BRIDAL COUTURE
by Susan Khalje
This volume is a great reference book, even if you never plan to sew bridal dresses. The techniques are useful; I use this book often for standard dressmaking.

COUTURE SEWING TECHNIQUES
by Claire B. Shaeffer
This book explains many essential couture sewing techniques and has spectacular photos of garments.

FIT AND PATTERNMAKING BOOKS

PATTERNMAKING FOR FASHION DESIGN
by Helen Joseph-Armstrong
This book was one of my textbooks in fashion design school and I still refer to it. If you want to learn about flat pattern drafting, this is the book to get!

FIT FOR REAL PEOPLE
by Pati Palmer and Marta Alto
Covering the basics on how to adjust patterns for a better fit, this book walks you through tissue-fitting a pattern and adjusting patterns for your body.

FABRIC RESOURCES

There are tons of great fabric resources out there—more than I can list! Here are some of my favorites, including places I visited to find the fabrics used in this book.

BRITEX FABRICS
If you live in or visit the San Francisco Bay Area, this store is a must-see. They also have a limited selection of items available online.
www.britexfabrics.com

DENVER FABRICS
A go-to online fabric retailer.
www.denverfabrics.com

EMMA ONE SOCK
Online fabric retailer selling high-end designer fabrics, from wovens to knits.
emmaonesock.com

ETSY
A great online marketplace for sourcing vintage and new fabrics.
www.etsy.com

FABRIC.COM
If you want a big selection, this is the online fabric resource for you.
fabric.com

HART'S FABRIC
A wonderful store in Santa Cruz, California, that sells all types of fabrics. If you can't make it in person, they carry stock online, too.
www.hartsfabric.com

JO-ANN FABRIC AND CRAFT STORES
A chain fabric and craft store found in most major U.S. cities.
www.joann.com

MARCY TILTON
A wonderful online resource for knit fabrics. They carry other fabrics as well, but I have had the best luck purchasing great knits from them.
marcytilton.com

MOOD FABRICS
Made famous by Project Runway, Mood has stores in both New York City and Los Angeles. They also offer a wide selection of fabrics online.
www.moodfabrics.com

THRIFT STORES
Thrift stores can be hit or miss, but I have scored many nice fabrics at local thrift stores. I find that the smaller thrift stores, run by local charities, have the best selection of sewing and craft supplies.

BLOGS

There are so many sewing blogs out there at any given time, I certainly can't keep up with them all. But here is a list of some of my favorites that I read pretty regularly.

COLETTERIE
The Coletterie is the blog for the Colette pattern company. It is a wonderful blog that has sewing tutorials, tips, and inspiring photos.
www.coletterie.com

ELEGANT MUSINGS
Casey shares her love of vintage fashion, sewing, and her fantastic sense of style on her charming blog.
blog.caseybrowndesigns.com

FRABJOUS COUTURE
This blog is run by couture enthusiast Marina, who displays her beautiful couture creations and offers good technical information on sewing and patterns.
www.coutureschmiede.com

GERTIE'S NEW BLOG FOR BETTER SEWING
Gertie blogs about her sewing adventures by showing you the lovely garments she makes, giving great tutorials and sewing inspiration.
www.blogforbettersewing.com

MADALYNNE
Madalynne's blog has some really great pattern-making tutorials and offers all sorts of sewing-related tidbits.
www.madalynne.com

SEW, MAMA, SEW!
A great resource for all types of sewing, fabric information, sew-alongs, and tutorials.
sewmamasew.com

SIS BOOM
Fabric designer, author, and general crafty lady Jennifer Paganelli blogs about her crafty life and shares a lot of creations that folks have made with her fabric.
www.sisboom.com/blog/

THE SEW WEEKLY
Such a rich site and blog, which has weekly clothing sewing challenges, an active community of fellow sewing enthusiasts, and gets you in the mood to sew.
www.sewweekly.com

ACKNOWLEDGMENTS

I am so thankful and grateful to the many people that were involved in making this book possible.

To my editor, Laura Lee Mattingly: without your vision and encouragement this book would not have seen the light of day. Thank you for thinking of me for the project.

To the designer, Jennifer Tolo Pierce: you made this book so elegantly beautiful and I truly love how it turned out.

To the technical editor, Diane Neer, and the copy editor, Ellen Wheat: your technical skills and insight truly made this book better.

To the rest of the Chronicle Books team: you publish wonderful books and I feel so honored to be one of your authors.

To the photographer, Daniel Castro, and his team, Karishma, Marc, and Geary: thank you for the stunning photos that capture the feeling of this book so perfectly.

Thank you to hair stylist William Soriano and his team; makeup artist Preston Nesbit and his team; and our gorgeous models, Alexis, Delana, and Jillian.

I am also thankful to have such wonderful friends and family.

To my mom: thanks for exposing me to the many different fiber arts. I grew up watching you sew and I couldn't wait to sew my own clothes. Look where it got me!

To my dad, Janet, Sara, Katie, Bobbe, Rosemarie, Ken, Louise, Guy, and Lyla: your love and support mean the world to me.

To Erin McGee, the best boss-lady and good friend: I knew we were kindred spirits when you hired me. I miss Bobbin's Nest but I am so glad I still have you in my life.

To Jennifer Paganelli: you are an inspiration. Thank you for giving me the confidence to write my own book.

To my group of talented and fabulous girlfriends, Karen, Irene, Sarah, Andy, Olivia, and Natalie: you are all so special to me. Thanks for making me laugh.

And an extra special huge THANK YOU to my kind and oh-so-patient husband, Matthew. Without you I could not have written this book. You went through all the highs and lows and kept me somewhat sane. I am so lucky to have you and our two silly dogs, Mikey and Butternut.

INDEX

Photo Credits

Page 44: Photo by Lipnitzki/Roger Viollet/Getty Images
Page 56: MGM/The Kobal Collection/George Hurrell/Art Resource, NY
Page 70: Rex USA/Moviestore Collection/Rex
Page 84: Rex USA/SNAP/Rex
Page 96: Paramount/The Kobal Collection/Art Resource, NY
Page 108: Photo by Keystone-France/Gamma-Keystone/Getty Images
Page 124: Photo by Gene Lester/Getty Images
Page 136: Photo by Time & Life Pictures/Getty Images
Page 146: Photo by Tim Graham/Getty Images
Page 158: Photo by Dave M. Benett/Getty Images